the **wonder weeks**
Milestone Guide

**Your Baby's Development, Sleep, and
Crying Explained**

This book is dedicated to my daughter, Xaviera. I couldn't have done it without her. This book is also dedicated to my grandchildren, Thomas, Victoria, and Sarah, who have taught me a lot.

WITHDRAWN

the Wonder Weeks

Milestone Guide

Your Baby's Development, Sleep and
Crying Explained

WORLDWIDE
BEST-SELLING
BABY APP
#1

 Based on 35 years of research

 The Wonder Weeks series: over 2 million sold worldwide

 Doctor recommended

Xaviera Plas and Frans Plooij, Ph.D.

Copyright © Kiddy World Publishing
Written by: Xaviera Plas and Frans Plooij
Internal Design by: Andrei Andras
Cover Design by: Bastiaan Leideritz
Illustrations: Hetty van de Rijt, Vladimir Schmeisser

ISBN/EAN: 978-94-91882-13-5

Kiddy World Publishing
Van Pallandtstraat 63
6814 GN Arnhem
The Netherlands
www.thewonderweeks.com

Like us on Facebook! facebook.com/WonderWeeks
Follow us on Twitter: twitter.com/TheWonderWeeks
Printed in Canada

CONTENTS

PHYSICAL DEVELOPMENT

PREAMBLE

Congratulations! You've become a proud mother or father (again) of a cute baby. For months, you've been longing for the moment when you would finally hold your baby in your arms, cuddle and talk to your child, and admire his or her tiny feet. There's nothing better than becoming parents. From now on, you are a team, a great unity. You want to do everything right, which brings, no doubt, a whole bunch of worries and questions with it. The questions and doubts are perfectly normal. They are even good to have. They bring out the best in you, and this is to your baby's advantage.

Over the years, parents have asked me lots of questions on all kinds of subjects. They are questions that are not only on these parents' minds but that are interesting to every father and mother. I hope to answer all of your questions with this book. Happy reading!

Frans Plooij

DEFINITIONS

GROWTH SPURT

- You talk about a growth spurt when the body, or a part of the body, suddenly becomes bigger or changes. Sometimes, children grow several millimeters a night and then, for a while, not at all. "Children grow like weeds" goes the saying, and they really do.

- The head circumference grows in spurts as well. The head circumference's first three growth spurts after birth coincide with the first three leaps in the baby's mental development.

- Other growth spurts rarely concur with leaps because they occur much more frequently. The baby also doesn't start teething during a leap.

LEAP

A leap is a sudden change in the baby's mental development. Usually, it comes with the same symptoms every time; your baby is especially clingy, whiny, and moody. Leaps announce progress. In healthy children, they occur 10 times within the first 20 months after birth at approximately the same age. They are more intense in some children than in others. Every leap brings a change in the brain, broadening the perceptive ability by another skill.

SKILLS

When a child's cognitive ability increases with a leap, he or she is able to learn a whole bunch of new skills and new behavior that the child didn't know before since the brain wasn't ready for it then. The new behavior is the result of tireless work. It doesn't just fall into the child's lap, but the baby has to work hard for it. Every skill requires practicing, and practicing requires time. Your baby starts the process of acquiring a new skill when it suits him or her. The child makes the call and can't acquire all skills at the same time. That's why the age when a new behavior appears varies from child to child.

PERCEPTIVE ABILITY

Each leap brings your baby a new cognitive ability. It is a present to the baby, who doesn't have to do anything to receive it. Within the first 20 months, your baby acquires 10 cognitive abilities. Each extension of the cognitive ability is the result of a sudden change in the brain. It happens at around the same age for every child. Each extension of the cognitive ability provides the baby with a brand-new option to learn. This means that your baby is able to learn a whole new range of skills. These skills are all due to the new perceptive ability, and the baby couldn't have learned them before the appearance of the new perceptive ability. The new perceptive abilities that are, one by one, available to the baby during the first 20 months are "sensations," "patterns," "smooth transitions," "events," "relationships," "categories," "sequences," "programs," "principles," and "systems." These perceptive abilities are explained in detail in the book, *The Wonder Weeks.*

Chapter 1

MENTAL DEVELOPMENT

Leaps, Working the Brain,
Clinginess, Whininess, and
Moodiness

As parents, you are very interested in what happens inside your baby's little head. What does the baby experience? How is the child feeling? What does or doesn't the baby understand? Why does the baby consider something to be very funny? Of course, you can't ask your child yet, so all you can do is read behavior and body language. Knowing your baby's mental development makes it a lot easier to understand your baby.

WHY IS MENTAL DEVELOPMENT SO IMPORTANT?

We tend to mainly look at visible results. Is the baby able to walk? Is he or she able to talk? Of course, it's great to experience the first milestone, but the process that takes place before the milestone is really what's important and interesting. In order to be able to perform an action, no matter what it is, the brain has to be able to communicate with the body. The brain has to be capable of receiving signals from the outside world, translating them, and then stimulating the body to "do something." If the brain is not capable of receiving signals from the outside world, it can't translate or stimulate either. Adults, for instance, know that you have to lift your foot to climb a step because you know that the step is higher up than the floor you're standing on. A little baby doesn't understand the consequences of height differences yet. The baby sees the step but doesn't understand what a step requires until the brain develops this ability during a mental leap. Once the mental leap is complete, the baby is suddenly better able to handle height differences. As a Mom or a Dad, you see the outcome, and you're proud of it. Your baby is able to do something new. However, it is very important to realize that the true milestone happened in the brain during mental development. Everything we do and know is determined by our mental development.

WHAT EXACTLY IS A LEAP, ANYWAY?

A leap in your baby's mental development means a big, sudden change in your baby's little head. The brain is now capable of perceiving things that it couldn't perceive before. The change is so large that the baby's whole world seems different now.

HOW DOES MY BABY'S WORLD CHANGE WHEN HE OR SHE TAKES A LEAP IN HIS OR HER MENTAL DEVELOPMENT?

With each leap your baby takes, a new cognitive ability is acquired. This new ability enables the baby to perceive, see, hear, taste, smell, and feel new things. Everything the baby notices now is new even though it has been in his or her surroundings for quite a while. The baby hasn't noticed it until now because the brain wasn't able to understand it. From the moment the baby takes the leap, this changes, and suddenly, the baby sees all the new things he or she is surrounded by. It's difficult for adults to imagine, but the baby's whole world changes because of it.

WHAT IS THE BABY'S REACTION TO A LEAP?

During a leap, the baby's world is briefly upside down. The best way to describe it is to compare it to waking up on a different planet. You open your eyes, and everything has changed. What would you do? Frightened, you hang on to what you're used to and what you know. Slowly, you start exploring the new planet. That's exactly what your baby does. He or she hangs on to you, appearing clingy. However, you don't only see the effect of a leap in the exaggerated clinginess of your baby, but you'll also notice more mood swings and crying. Clinginess, whininess, and moodiness are the constant companions of every leap your child takes.

Do remember

If all this terminology is making you dizzy, turn to page 14, chapter "Definitions."

WHAT ARE THE CONSEQUENCES FOR THE BABY OF ACQUIRING A NEW COGNITIVE ABILITY?

The new ability that your baby gains during a leap gives your baby the potential to develop a whole series of skills, which can be divided into different groups according to their similarities. Compare it to a supermarket with different departments containing related products. Your baby is able to enter a certain department at a supermarket for the first time. A product has to be chosen, and you can't buy everything in that department all at once. What is chosen and how your baby uses it is what makes your baby unique.

IS MY BABY GOING TO MASTER EVERYTHING RIGHT AWAY AFTER TAKING A LEAP IN HIS OR HER DEVELOPMENT?

When your baby has taken a leap in development, it means that the baby has made room for a new cognitive ability. The baby is not as whiny, clingy, or moody. Of course, this doesn't mean that the baby masters every single one of the skills that the new ability allows. The baby's little brain is basically ready for a whole range of new behavior, but this requires practice. Your baby learns by experiencing, by making mistakes, and by tireless trying. Practice takes a lot of time. Your baby is able to master some of the skills shortly after the leap but others take longer. The skills they master shortly after the leap are different for each baby.

WHAT NEEDS TO BE CONSIDERED IN REGARDS TO PROCESSING A LEAP?

After a leap has taken place, it has to be processed first. This is the period of time during which your baby tries to get a grip on the new possibilities. During this phase, parents learn a lot about their child's personality. Pay attention to the following:

○ How does your baby handle being unsuccessful when trying something?

○ Which ones of the new things does the baby find the most interesting and learns the quickest?

HOW DOES THE BABY HANDLE BEING UNSUCCESSFUL WHEN TRYING SOMETHING NEW?

After a leap, your baby will try out all kinds of new things pertaining to the extended cognitive ability, but of course, your baby will not try all of them at once. Often times, your baby will wait months in between trying new things. Needless to say, not all the attempts the child makes in trying to master a skill are successful. The saying, "practice makes perfect," also applies to babies. One baby patiently tries over and over until success is found. Another baby quickly gets mad and frustrated when something doesn't work out and doesn't try again. Another baby reacts with frustration if unsuccessful but eagerly keeps trying until it works out. In addition to these, there are many more reactions to an initially unsuccessful attempt. If you pay attention to the course of attempts, you'll see part of your baby's personality shimmer through. You get an idea of how your child handles failure and achievement of goals. The behavior is very revealing, especially since your child hasn't learned to behave reasonably yet. The baby doesn't pull him- or herself together, doesn't swallow anger, and reacts in a very pristine manner.

When your baby processes a leap, write down how he or she practices new skills. The left-hand side of the bar indicates that your baby goes about trying something new in an even-tempered frame of mind without losing his or her patience while the right-hand side indicates a pretty high degree of frustration. During the processing of a leap, color the part of the bar that you think describes your baby. Do this as unbiasedly as possible. Your baby's ability to handle something with patience has its advantages, but your baby is also justified in losing his or her patience and being frustrated. Therefore, one behavior is not better than the other.

LEAP 1: 5 WEEKS

even tempered	frustrated

LEAP 2: 8 WEEKS

even tempered	frustrated

LEAP 3: 12 WEEKS

even tempered	frustrated

LEAP 4: 19 WEEKS

even tempered	frustrated

LEAP 5: 26 WEEKS

even tempered	frustrated

LEAP 6: 37 WEEKS

even tempered	frustrated

LEAP 7: 46 WEEKS

even tempered	frustrated

LEAP 8: 55 WEEKS

even tempered	frustrated

LEAP 9: 64 WEEKS

even tempered	frustrated

LEAP 10: 75 WEEKS

even tempered	frustrated

WHICH ONE OF THE NEW SKILLS DOES THE BABY FIND THE MOST INTERESTING?

This book tells you what your baby may learn during each individual leap. With each leap in development, the baby acquires a whole range of new possibilities. The baby is able to do and understand so many new things that only one can be selected. It's simply impossible to practice and master all of them at the same time. Once again, use the supermarket for comparison. Hundreds of products are being offered there. Which ones do you put in your shopping basket? You reach for the products that appeal to you. Your baby does the same thing when processing a leap. Among all the skills that are being offered, your baby picks the ones that are appealing; in other words, your baby picks the ones he or she has a preference for. The baby's preferences always reveal something about his or her personality.

HOW DO YOU DISCOVER YOUR CHILD'S PERSONALITY?

You get a pretty good picture of his or her personality by being responsive to everything your baby "tells" you with body language and by carefully observing your baby. If, on top of that, you document what your baby chooses from the "supermarket" of possibilities, you get an even better picture. Some parents tend to put everything a baby is able to do on their "must-have list," which is a shame because it makes it seem like having to fill the shopping cart is the priority. It really isn't about crossing off as many skills as possible, but instead, it's about tracking your baby's preferences (also see chapter 8, "Intelligence," page 131).

WHAT PHASE FOLLOWS THE PROCESSING OF A LEAP?

The next leap comes shortly after your baby has somewhat processed a leap and learned a number of new skills. Your baby's life changes drastically once again. This happens 10 times during the first 20 months, mainly within the first three months because leaps are more frequent during this period.

Of course, your baby is far from mastering all the potential skills of the previous leap when the next leap begins. No reason to worry, though; the baby simply continues mastering skills and doesn't pay attention to the new leap. Therefore, completely processing all the potential skills of one leap overlaps a series of other leaps.

ONCE MY BABY HAS MASTERED A SKILL, DOES IT CHANGE EVER AGAIN?

A new cognitive ability that was acquired with a new leap enables your baby to improve a previously mastered skill or to do more with it. You could compare it to building a house. First, you build the foundation and then the walls and then the roof, and finally, you divide the house into rooms and furnish it. You can't put a roof on a house that doesn't have walls. Your baby builds on the foundation of mental development. With every leap, the baby adds a level.

Your baby not only learns more skills per leap but also learns that the skills acquired before can be used in different ways. With every leap, the child learns to use previous accomplishments in a more creative way. Take, for example, "grabbing." The first time your baby was able to get a hold of something happened pretty tediously and with little control.

The baby's movements seemed robotic. You were holding the toy and made sure that the baby's hand got close to the toy. A few leaps later, the baby reaches for an object lying around and moves it to a different place. As you can see, the grabbing has turned into a resource. Grabbing itself is not the goal anymore but a means to achieve something else. The end goal has moved up a level. The baby's little hand now makes smooth movements, and the baby understands how to "navigate." The skills the baby has acquired while processing a leap have been refined (see also chapter 2, "Physical Development," page 33).

WHEN DOES A CHILD TAKE A LEAP IN HIS OR HER DEVELOPMENT?

All children take their leaps at the same age. Always take the calculated date of delivery as a starting point. It's about the development of the brain. Whether your baby was born a few weeks earlier or later, the development of the brain simply proceeds. The chart on page 28 shows when your child will take a leap.

WHY DO ALL CHILDREN TAKE A LEAP AT THE SAME TIME? EVERY CHILD IS DIFFERENT, RIGHT?

All children take leaps at the same age because the leap's trigger comes from the inside; the surroundings don't have any influence on it. This doesn't mean that all children handle each leap in the same manner. Every child handles the newly acquired expansion of perceptive ability differently, which is exactly what makes each child unique.

DO I HAVE TO ADJUST MY SCHEDULE ACCORDINGLY IF A NEW LEAP IS ABOUT TO HAPPEN?

Most certainly, your child doesn't feel well during a leap. However, the severity of bewilderment is hard to estimate. Since the child takes so many leaps during the first two years, you won't always be able to take off during that time, of course. It's not necessary, but you should be somewhat considerate. For example, don't make an appointment for shots at the pediatrician's office during the days of a leap. If you can schedule important appointments before or after a leap, you should do so.

WHY CAN YOU CLEARLY TELL WHEN SOME BABIES ARE TAKING LEAPS BUT NOT OTHERS?

You may look at a leap in terms of a big change. Some adults have a stronger reaction to changes in life than others. It's the same with babies. To some children, handling changes comes naturally and is easier than it is for others. Besides temper, these influencing factors play a role as well:

○ Stressful situations

○ Health

If you are, for example, in the middle of moving your family, if your daily life is influenced by some other stressful event, or if your baby is sick, the leap is overcast by these circumstances. Your baby is especially clingy due to the situation, which makes the leap that's about to happen less obvious.

YOUR BABY'S 10 GREAT FUSSY PHASES

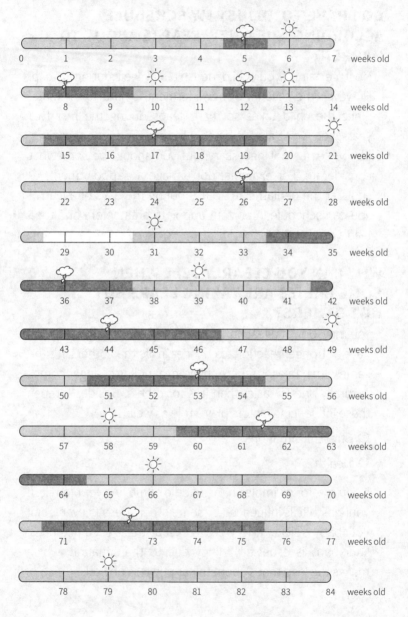

More than likely, you're experiencing a phase where your baby is relatively easy going.

☐ If your baby is especially clingy at the age of 29 and 30 weeks and is whiny and moody, it doesn't necessarily indicate another leap. Your baby has simply discovered that you can walk away and leave him or her alone. As strange as it may sound, this is progress! Your child is learning about distances and is, therefore, acquiring a new skill.

■ Your baby may be clingier at this time.

⛆ Right around this time, you'll probably experience some rough times.

☀ Right around this week, your baby is probably the sunshine of the house.

DOES A BABY GET SICK MORE OFTEN DURING A LEAP?

Many babies don't get sick during the leap but do shortly after. This is because they have to process so many new things that they're prone to illnesses. Your baby doesn't sleep well during this difficult time, eats less, and doesn't feel well. These are the ingredients for getting sick. T. Berry Brazelton, a famous pediatrician, has observed that parents come to his office considerably more often after their child has taken a leap. However, illnesses should generally never be underestimated. If you are concerned about your baby's health, you need to see a pediatrician immediately. It's probably nothing, but it's better to be safe than sorry.

WHY ARE SOME LEAPS MORE DIFFICULT FOR THE BABY THAN OTHERS?

You'll notice that your baby acts clingier, whinier, and moodier during some leaps but less so during others. This may be connected to your baby finding the skills that come with these leaps especially interesting, or the child wasn't feeling well when the leap started. Always keep in mind that it's perfectly normal when one leap is more difficult for your baby than another. This is no reason for concern. Try to figure out why your baby reacts more severely to a certain leap, and help your baby when he or she has a hard time with a leap.

HOW CAN I HELP MY BABY GET THROUGH A LEAP?

Taking and processing a leap can only be done by the baby. You can't make it more comfortable for the baby, but you can certainly make it easier. You can do this by:

- ○ Exposing your baby to situations that stimulate the new perceptive ability
- ○ Making sure your baby gets well-deserved rest in time

One week before your baby takes a leap, read the chapter in this book pertaining to the leap. That way, you'll know what your baby will soon be interested in, so you can prepare and offer everything he or she needs. You're helping the baby process the impressions of the leap simply by enabling him or her to discover a new world. All the new impressions the baby receives during a leap take a lot of energy; therefore, your baby will need to rest. Sometimes, just a short nap will do, but other times, the baby may want to sleep for a few hours.

You are the one who can tell best when your baby needs rest. By arranging for rest in a timely manner, you make it easier for the baby to process a leap.

DOES A SMART CHILD DO EVERYTHING RIGHT AFTER A LEAP THAT HE OR SHE HAS THE CAPABILITY OF DOING?

As soon as your baby has completed a leap in mental development, he or she is able to do certain things that he or she simply wasn't able to do before. With the new cognitive ability, the child is capable of learning a spectrum of new skills. The spectrum is so large and includes so many new things that there's no way for your child to do everything at the same time. Your baby acquired the new ability without having asked for it because he or she is at the age where the brain makes the ability possible.

Without having asked for it, the child is now able to do hundreds of new things, which doesn't mean that all will be mastered at once. The saying, "practice makes perfect," pertains to everything in life. Your baby will try out a few new things on his or her own, that appeal to him or her. The subconscious selection of some of the many skills is the starting point. Your child will, then, practice, practice, practice until the skill(s) are mastered. At this point, the child will pick out something else from all the new options and start practicing.

The number of new things your baby chooses after completing a leap doesn't reveal anything at all about intelligence, so don't consider the list with new possible skills that pertain to each leap to be a check-off list. Resist the urge of making this into a to-do list. No baby in this world is able to do everything at once. Be fair to yourself and to your baby. Look at the things the baby is fascinated with and what new things the baby wants to try out. That way, you cater to your baby, giving him or her self-confidence and a solid foundation for secure bonds (see also Chapter 6, "Emotional Development," page 103).

ARE THERE LEAPS WHILE THE BABY IS STILL IN THE WOMB AS WELL AS AFTER THE 10TH LEAP?

Human beings take mental leaps their whole life, so they probably occur while still in the womb. Think of puberty and the midlife crisis. When you're right in the midst of them, you don't consider them to be fun, but they're, ultimately, defining periods in life. Our development never comes to a standstill.

Chapter 2

PHYSICAL DEVELOPMENT

Gross Motor Skills,
Fine Motor Skills,
Growth, and Reflexes

During the first years of a baby's life, mainly within the first 12 months, a lot happens but not only in your child's head; the baby discovers his or her body and learns to use it. Within a year and a half, the little one changes from a baby that's born with a number of reflexes to a toddler, who grabs things, crawls, or even walks. The child is getting bigger and increasingly stronger and uses his or her body better.

IS IT TRUE THAT CHILDREN ALSO GO THROUGH PHYSICAL GROWTH SPURTS?

Every parent can tell you a thing or two about his or her child's clothes suddenly being too small. Children literally outgrow their clothes from one day to the next. The physical growth spurts and the mental leaps have something in common; they happen suddenly and unannounced. However, they don't happen at the same time.

DO THE REFLEXES THE BABY IS BORN WITH DISAPPEAR DURING THE LEAPS?

You probably know that there is a whole series of inherent reflexes. Reactions take place right after the baby's birth without the baby having to think about them. Some are controlled by the midwife or doctor present at the delivery. What many people don't know is that the inherent reflexes vanish and are replaced by other reflexes! The vanishing of reflexes and the development of new ones, however, don't happen in connection with a leap.

DOES TEETHING COINCIDE WITH LEAPS?

The age at which a baby is teething greatly varies. Teething, therefore, doesn't have anything to do with leaps in development. The picture below shows you which teeth usually emerge when.

Teething doesn't necessarily happen during the leaps

The picture shows you the order in which teeth usually erupt. However, babies aren't machines. Your baby gets his or her first tooth when it's ready. It's a matter of disposition. How long it takes for the teeth to appear and how much time there is between the appearances of each tooth doesn't reveal anything about your baby's health or stage of development.

Bright babies may get their teeth early or late, quickly or slowly.

In most cases, the first tooth breaks through the gum when the baby is six months old. It's the two bottom front teeth (1). Most times, the child has six teeth when celebrating his or her first birthday. At the age of two and a half years, the last molars (8) appear and complete the primary set of teeth. At that time, the toddler has 20 teeth.

Below, you may record the dates and sequence in which your baby's teeth appear.

Caution: Diarrhea and/or fever don't have anything to do with teething. If your baby has these symptoms, it's usually a sign of sickness.

DATE:

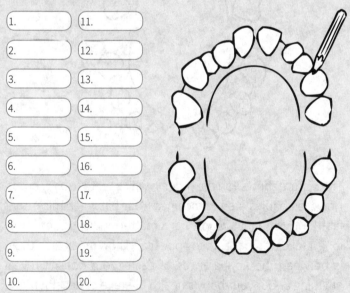

1.	11.
2.	12.
3.	13.
4.	14.
5.	15.
6.	16.
7.	17.
8.	18.
9.	19.
10.	20.

DOES THE HEAD CIRCUMFERENCE ALSO CHANGE DURING LEAPS?

There are, indeed, certain stages in life during which the head suddenly grows in circumference. This often happens before a leap in mental development. It happens for the first time approximately after three weeks, when your baby is seven or eight weeks, at 11 weeks, and at around 15 weeks. Anything beyond that hasn't been measured.

Just as with the leaps in mental development, you have to use the calculated delivery date as the starting point, not the actual date of birth. The baby's brain doesn't grow any faster if the baby is born too early or slower if he or she stays in your belly for 42 weeks.

WHAT KIND OF PHYSICAL DEVELOPMENTS ARE THERE, AND WHY IS THIS NOT THE SAME IN ALL BABIES?

Everything your baby does with his or her body falls under physical development and is distinguished between gross motor skills (holding up the head, turning around, sitting, grabbing, crawling, walking, running, etc.) and fine motor skills (reaching for something specific, holding a pen, pushing a button, doing a puzzle, etc.). If a child is more interested in gross motor skills, he or she will focus on quickly mastering these skills. A child who's more interested in fine motor skills will do everything it takes to learn all of the things in this category. What's noticeable is that children who mainly like observing are also often interested in fine motor skills, so don't exclusively pay attention to the gross motor skills when studying your baby's physical development.

WHICH ONE IS MORE IMPORTANT: FINE MOTOR SKILLS OR GROSS MOTOR SKILLS?

We need both in life; therefore, you can't say that one is more important than the other. The important thing is that you give your baby the opportunity to practice both. Play games that promote the gross motor skills and games where the focus is on the fine motor skills. However, always let your baby decide whether or not he or she wants to play a game. Babies won't learn anything when forced to play a game they don't feel like playing. Even worse, they will develop a dislike towards the game.

DOES THE DEVELOPMENT OF GROSS MOTOR SKILLS TAKE PLACE AT THE SAME AGE IN ALL BABIES?

To many people, what counts first and foremost are clearly visible end results. That's why parents are often asked, "Is the child walking yet?" or "The child is not crawling yet?" All of these questions are completely redundant and may even upset you. Always keep in mind that a child does something only when he or she is ready for it, and the point in time when the child is ready doesn't reveal anything about intelligence or development. Parents may find it comforting to know that the point in time a baby is able to sit, stand, crawl, or walk may vary greatly. It is also good to know the earliest point in time your baby will be able to perform a certain action. The earliest expected time the child will be able to learn something new is determined by the leaps in mental development. Of course, the child has to have the mental ability for a certain movement before being able to control his or her body.

MOTOR MILESTONES		
Behavior	Average Age (Approximate)	Range of ages
(A) Head control when held to shoulder		
Lifts head	Neonatal period	
Makes postural adjustment	Neonatal period	
Head erect - vertical	3 weeks	9 days - 3 months
Head erect - steady	7 weeks	3 weeks - 4 months
Holds head steady	2½ months	1 month - 5 months
Head balanced	4 months, 1 week	2 months - 6 months
(B) Motor behaviors in prone position		
Lateral head movements	Neonatal period	
Crawling movements	By 2 weeks	Neonatal period - 3 months
Elevates self by arms	Just after 2 months	3 weeks - 5 months
Able to progress (move) in some fashion	Just after 7 months	5 months - 11 months
(C) Motor behaviors in supine position or on side		
Thrusts arms in play	3½ weeks	9 days - 2 months
Thrusts legs in play	3½ weeks	9 days - 2 months
Holds on to large plastic ring	3½ weeks	9 days - 3 months
Lifts head (dorsal suspension)	1 month, 3 weeks	3 weeks - 4 months
Turns from side to side	By 2 months	3 weeks - 5 months
Turns from back to side	2½ months	2 months - 7 months

Source: Collaborative Perinatal Research Projet form of the Bayley tests

WALKING,* STANDING BALANCE, AND STAIR-CLIMBING BEHAVIORS

Behavior	Average Age (Approximate)	Range of ages
(A) Walking		
Early stepping movements	7 months, 2 weeks	5 months - 11 months
Stepping movements	8 months, 3 weeks	6 months - 12 months
Walks with help	9½+ months	7 months - 12 months
Sits down	9½+ months	7 months - 14 months
Stands alone	11 months	9 months - 16 months
Walks alone	11 months, 3 weeks	9 months - 17 months
(B) Balance		
Stands on right foot with help	16 months	12 months - 21 months
Stands on left foot with help	16+ months	12 months - 23 months
Stands on left foot alone	22 months, 3 weeks	15 months - 30+ months
Stands on right foot alone	23½ months	16 months - 30+ months
Jumps off floor, both feet	By 23½ months	17 months - 30+ months
(C) Stair climbing		
Walks up strairs with help	16+ months	12 months - 23 months
Walks down stairs with help	By 16½ months	13 months - 23 months
Walks up stairs alone, both feet on each step	25+ months	18 months - 30+ months
Walks down stairs alone, both feet on each step	25 months, 3 weeks	19 months - 30+ months
Walks up stairs alternating forward foot	30+ months	23 months - 30+ months

*including motoric control when standing

Source: Collaborative Perinatal Research Projet form of the Bayley tests

SITTING BEHAVIORS AND EFFORTS TO ACHIEVE A VERTICAL POSITION

Behavior	Average Age (Approximate)	Range of ages
(A) Placed by adult		
Sits with support	2 months, 1 week	1 months - 5 months
Sits with slight support	3 months, 3 weeks	2 months - 6 months
Sits alone, momentarily	5 months, 1 week	4 months - 8 months
Sits alone, 30 seconds or more	6 months	5 months - 8 months
Sits alone, steady	6½ months	5 months - 9 months
Sits alone, good coordination	7 months	5 months - 10 months
(B)Helped by adult		
Makes effort to sit	4 months, 3 weeks	3 months - 8 months
Pulls to sitting	5 months, 3 weeks	4 months - 8 months
Pulls to standing	8 months	5 months - 12 months
(C) Helped by furniture		
Raises self to sitting	8 months, 1 week	6 months -11 months
Stand up alone	8½ months	6 months - 12 months
Stands up, level I	12½ months	9 months - 18 months
Stands up, level II	By 22 months	11 months - 30+ months
Stands up, level III	30+ months	22 months - 30+ months

Source: Collaborative Perinatal Research Projet form of the Bayley tests

SHOULD I BE WORRIED IF MY BABY DOESN'T LEARN SOMETHING QUICKLY IN REGARDS TO GROSS MOTOR SKILLS?

The brain controls the body, so a baby has to be capable of doing something with the brain before being able to control the body. In this book, we're describing at what point in time the brain is able to set the body in motion, which is the earliest expected time your baby is capable of performing a certain action. This pertains to the development of the baby's gross motor skills as well as the fine motor skills. Whether the baby is going to do it or not depends on a variety of factors, including:

○ How interested the baby is in the things he or she is able to do with the gross motor or the fine motor skills

○ Whether the body is able to perform what the brain wants

WHY DO SOME BABIES CRAWL AND WALK SOONER THAN OTHERS?

Some babies are simply not interested in crawling or walking. Some babies are more interested in, for example, spatial aspects provided by stacking games and interlocking plastic bricks. This may engross their mind completely. These little ones won't try very hard when learning to walk either; they would rather do something else. They start crawling or walking once it's a resource for them to achieve something else such as when they want a certain building brick that they can't otherwise get to. Then, they try crawling to get to the object. Their goal is not the crawling itself but getting their hands on the brick.

Compare it to buying a car. Some people buy a pretty, luxurious car because they like driving it. Others aren't interested in what kind of car it is as long as it takes them from A to B.

Babies who are interested in gross motor skills will start crawling and walking considerably sooner than babies who aren't interested in those activities. It makes sense because you don't do anything you're not interested in. These babies are going to try anything to learn a new acrobatic trick as soon as their mental development permits it. They practice and practice until they are able to stand, crawl, or walk. They enjoy the physical activity and are proud and beam with joy when they succeed.

One group of babies is not better or smarter than the other. It is very important that you, as parents, always react positively and intensively towards your baby's interests. Observe the child attentively and listen to what he or she is "telling" you whether with words or body language. Never force your baby to do something he or she has absolutely no interest in.

HOW SHOULD I REACT WHEN MY BABY WANTS TO TRY OUT GROSS MOTOR SKILLS BUT SIMPLY DOESN'T HAVE THE PHYSICAL ABILITY YET?

Sometimes, babies would love to sit, walk, or crawl, but they realize that their body doesn't obey. The result is frustration. The fact that your baby is mentally capable of sitting, crawling, and walking and is also interested in these skills doesn't necessarily mean that the baby is able to sit, crawl, and walk. You need your body for physical activity; however, sometimes, the body is not quite there yet. The muscles aren't strong enough or the body is still too heavy for its limited muscular strength. The frustration your baby shows is very understandable when wanting something, being excited about it, and feeling the urge to do something but being stuck in a body that doesn't comply.

Support your baby in his or her efforts by praising extensively. Encourage the baby, and assure him or her that he or she is doing a really good job. You'll notice that your child's frustration will dwindle. Also, you can help the child manage the physical "trick" by playing exercising games, but always stop as soon as you realize that it's getting to be too much for the little one.

CAN I HELP MY BABY WITH MASTERING PHYSICAL SKILLS?

Certainly, you can help, but don't force anything. The best way to help your child is to provide the opportunity and time needed to develop the skills. This holds true for all aspects of development. Do the necessary exercises with your child, and make sure the child can practice for the physical development. You, as the parents, have to provide the general conditions. Sometimes, you simply have to lay your child in a certain position; sometimes, you have to adjust something in the child's surroundings. The following table gives you an idea of what you should do.

WHAT TO PRACTICE	WHAT TO DO
Train neck muscles	Lay the baby on a soft blanket on his or her belly.
Learn using the body	Every once in a while, lay the baby down naked.
Learn grabbing	Hold a toy in front of the child to where he or she can easily grab it.
Sitting	Put the nursing pillow around the baby.
Crawling	Set your baby on a floor that's not too slick or hard.
Walking	○ Hold the child by his or her hand, or give the child some other kind of support. ○ Let your child go barefoot, or put antiskid socks on the child's feet.

WHY SHOULD YOU LEAVE THE BABY NAKED EVERY NOW AND THEN?

Clothes, no matter how soft they are, are still somewhat restricting. Clothes also prevent your baby from feeling his or her body. It's no different for babies than it is for us. Your baby finds it wonderful to lie around naked without restrictions. Get in the habit of giving your child this wonderful feeling every day. Needless to say, your child can't be lying in the way of a draft or on a cold floor because babies are very sensitive to cold temperatures.

HOW DO I SEE THAT IT'S GETTING TO BE TOO MUCH FOR MY BABY?

If you pay careful attention to your baby's signals, you know his or her boundaries. You see it in your baby's sleepy eyes or in his or her body, which is suddenly getting limper. Sometimes, the baby's hints are so subtle that only you are able to read them correctly, unlike the neighbor who doesn't see your child every day. If your baby is playing with somebody and you notice that it's getting to be too much, you should interfere. Always make sure that your baby doesn't get overexerted when playing an exercising game.

WHY IS IT SO IMPORTANT TO PAY ATTENTION TO THE BABY'S NECK?

The head is attached to the neck, and in babies, the head is relatively big compared to the body, much bigger than in adults. If adults still had the same proportions, our head would be almost as wide as our shoulders. So on top of your baby's small neck is a huge and heavy body part. If you take into consideration that the baby's neck muscles are not as developed as those of an adult's, it becomes obvious that it's hard work for your baby to lift his or her head and hold it upright. If your baby lifts his or her head and suddenly tilts it sideways, it can result in severe injuries. Don't ever underestimate this danger; always keep an eye on your baby's neck.

Below, you'll see the relation of human extremities throughout various stages of development. Do you see that the head of a baby is much larger in relation to the baby's legs compared to the body of an adult?

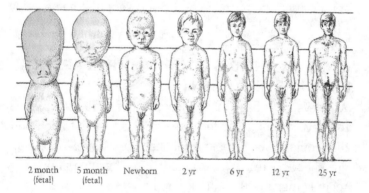

| 2 month (fetal) | 5 month (fetal) | Newborn | 2 yr | 6 yr | 12 yr | 25 yr |

Source: In the Beginning, p.311

Did you know? Between birth and adulthood:

- ○ the head becomes twice as big
- ○ the torso becomes three times as big
- ○ the arms become four times as big
- ○ the legs become five times as big

CAN BABIES OVERDO THEIR PHYSICAL TRAINING?

Most babies stop on their own when an exercising game is getting to be too much for them. You can tell by looking at some babies, though, that they're going beyond their limits. The little ones still have to learn to take a break when the exercise is getting to be too much. Your job, as parents, is to recognize your child's limits and protect the child from him- or herself. On the other hand, you also have to make sure to keep your own excitement at bay. You may find it exciting when your baby is sitting, turning, standing, crawling, or walking. However, if the child still has difficulty with it or is exhausted, you do more harm than good if you keep the game going. Don't ever force anything.

WHY IS MY CHILD'S BODY IS LIMPER AFTER A LEAP IN DEVELOPMENT?

Whenever your baby takes a leap, there's a brief step back in the development. Suddenly, the child isn't able to do things that could be done before the leap. Of course, this passes quickly, so there's no reason to worry. The child's body may seem limper, but the muscles and bones aren't. The child is just occupied with something else at the moment and briefly forgets how to use his or her body as before. A baby who's 18 weeks old and was pretty good at holding his or her head upright is, for instance, not able to do this anymore during the leap at around 26 weeks. This is the reason for little accidents, such as falls, during or shortly after a leap. Keep this in mind and be extra careful during this time.

CAN YOU SAY THAT THE BABY IS "HELPING" BY LIFTING THE BUTT DURING A DIAPER CHANGE?

Once your baby has taken the leap into "smooth transitions" (about 12 weeks after the calculated delivery date), you'll notice that the baby pushes up his or her butt during a diaper change. The child knows what's about to happen and beats you to it. As cute as this may seem and as handy as it is for you, it doesn't mean that your baby is trying to make it easier for you. Helping in order to please someone is a skill the baby won't have until around the age of 55 weeks.

WHEN IS THE BEST TIME TO START "PULLING-UP GAMES?"

Starting with the leap that takes place 12 weeks after the calculated delivery date, you may begin playing "pulling-up games" if your baby has a desire and the physical capability. Lay your child on his or her back in front of you, in your lap, or on a blanket on the floor. Take the child by the hands and stretch the little arms. That way, you basically invite the child to rise up to a sitting position. If your child tries to pull up, you may help a little bit. If the child doesn't make an effort to rise up, don't do anything. In this case, the child is simply not ready. Make sure to keep the baby's head from making nodding movements.

WHAT SHOULD YOU DO IF THE BABY DOESN'T WANT TO LIE IN THE STROLLER BUT WOULD RATHER LOOK AROUND?

Almost every stroller is equipped with multiple seat recline positions, so the child can lie flat or sit and admire the world. Starting at the age of six months, you may set your child in the stroller. You'll notice that after the leap of "relationships" (26 weeks, or six months, after the calculated delivery date), your child is not content anymore with just lying in the stroller. The little one wants to look at everything while being pushed in the stroller, so choose a stroller with an adjustable seat and set it on the lowest setting. As long as your walk doesn't last too long, the baby is able to handle this position well and receives food for the brain by being able to look at the surroundings.

MY BABY ALWAYS WANTS TO SIT WHEN IN THE STROLLER. ISN'T THIS TOO MUCH FOR THE CHILD?

Some babies are so curious about their surroundings that they simply can't get enough even if this means torturing their little bodies with all the sitting. A bouncer is ideal for these babies. Choose a bouncer that's adjustable, and pay attention to your baby's head when choosing a setting. If the head tilts sideways, you need to adjust the bouncer more towards a laying position. Adjust the bouncer regularly. Always keep an eye on your baby, and always pay attention to the posture of his or her head.

WHY DO SOME BABIES SCOOT BACKWARDS BEFORE REALLY CRAWLING FORWARD?

Not all babies scoot backwards before learning how to crawl. As soon the leap into "events" has been taken, the baby is capable of perceiving events, controlling them with his or her body, and learning skills such as crawling. Therefore, the baby could crawl if he or she desired to do so. However, it doesn't come easy to the child just like all the other skills. The skills literally have to be learned by falling down and getting back up. In doing so, babies try everything. You get to see the craziest techniques, and scooting backwards is one of them. Most times, this doesn't take long. You'll see that, within a week, your baby will try all kinds of variations. Once the little one discovers how to really crawl, it'll go quickly, and at that point, the child will let go of the other variations. Even if a baby has mastered crawling, you'll still get to see funny mistakes. For example, one baby had a pretty good idea about crawling but was still clearly in doubt about which hand (left or right) and which knee (left or right) to move. When the baby moved the right hand and the right knee at the same time, the little one fell over, of course. The result was angry screaming. Two days later, though, the baby was happily crawling around.

IS IT GOOD WHEN A BABY IS CRAWLING? IS THE BABY MISSING OUT WHEN HE OR SHE IS NOT CRAWLING?

Most babies crawl for a while before starting to walk. Others crawl only for a short period of time, and others skip crawling altogether. They may, for instance, scoot around in a sitting position or on the belly. Others only scoot backwards and turn around to move forward. There are some indications that it's good for a child's development to crawl in the classic way first before learning to walk. When crawling, the child sees the world in a different perspective, which is advantageous for the sense of vision and space. Of course, you can't force your child to crawl. You can encourage your little one, though, by playing crawling games and by making the surroundings "crawl friendly." A cold, hard floor that hurts the knees doesn't encourage crawling.

DO YOU HAVE TO PUT SHOES ON YOUR CHILD WHEN HE OR SHE IS LEARNING TO WALK?

Shoes were invented to protect our feet from the cold, dirt, and anything that could hurt, but they don't promote walking. Quite the opposite, your baby learns to use his or her feet better when barefoot or when wearing antiskid socks, which is the best option for indoors. There are special slippers that cover the little feet and ensure that they don't get cold. Buying these is a good idea for cold floors. You don't need to buy shoes until your child is running around outside. Always choose good-quality shoes. You may watch your pennies when buying luxury items but not when it comes to shoes. The important thing is that they provide good support, are soft, and offer enough space for your little one's feet to grow in them. At a good shoe store, you'll get advice and answers to your questions.

IS THERE A CONNECTION BETWEEN THE INTELLIGENCE QUOTIENT AND THE MASTERING OF FINE MOTOR SKILLS?

There is, in fact, a connection between the measurable IQ (also see Chapter 8, "Intelligence," page 131) and the fine motor skills. Although in little children IQ, EQ, or any other forms of intelligence cannot be measured with a test, it's proven that a higher or lower intelligence quotient at a later age coincides with a baby's fine motor skills. This relation was discovered when scientists did a Bayley test on a group of eight-month-old babies and observed their mental development, gross motor skills, and fine motor skills. Fine motor skills turned out to be the better indicator in estimating the IQ in a four-year-old child.

WHAT IS THE PROCESS OF DEVELOPING THE FINE MOTOR SKILL OF "GRABBING?"

Just as in the case of gross motor skills, you can't measure all babies by the same yardstick. Assuming the child will be given the opportunity, he or she will start doing something when the time is right, not sooner or later. "Grabbing" is a skill your baby will start practicing soon. As soon as the leap of "events" has taken place at 19 weeks, the child will be able to move his or her hand to where something can be grabbed. Refined grabbing will be learned at a later time. It calls for many months of practice for the baby to master this skill.

The following table (p. 55) shows you the development of "grabbing." You'll see the earliest expected point in time your baby is able to perform a certain action and the average age babies master a certain part of grabbing within this action.

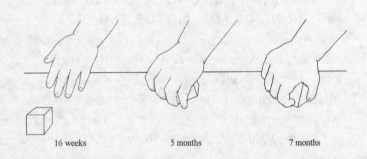

16 weeks   5 months   7 months

DO BABIES LEARN HOW TO USE THEIR HANDS AS SOON AS THEY'VE DISCOVERED THEM?

After the second leap at the age of eight weeks, your baby starts looking in amazement at the "things" that are attached to his or her arms. The child twists and turns his or her hands, frowns, and twists them again. The child sees that the hands are body parts but doesn't understand what to do with them until the third leap into "smooth transitions," which occurs 12 weeks after the calculated delivery date. At that time, you'll observe that your baby will try to grab something with his or her hands. It doesn't work all that well until the next leap. Once the next hurdle has been overcome, which is the leap of "events" occurring at 19 weeks after the calculated delivery date, the baby will be mentally able to hold on to something but will still need your help.

GRASPING OR HAND USAGE IN SITTING POSITION, AND FINE HAND CONTROL

Behavior	Average Age (Approximate)	Range of ages
(A) Grasping		
Grasps cube with ulnar-palm prehension (1-inch cube)	3 months, 3 weeks	2 months - 7 months
Grasps cube with partial thumb opposition	By 5 months	4 months - 8 months
Grasps cube with complete thumb opposition (radial-didital)	By 7 months	5 months - 9 months
(B) Manipulative capacity		
Reaches for objects, one hand only	By 5½ months	4 months - 8 months
Rotates wrist	5 months, 3 weeks	4 months - 8 months
Combines objects at midline (spoons or cubes)	8½ months	6 months - 10 months
Plays pat-a-cake with midline skill	9 months, 3 weeks	7 months - 15 months
(C) Smal pellet skill		
Attemps tosecure	5½ months	4 months - 8 months
Scoops	6 months, 3 weeks	5 months - 9 months
Grasps, partial finger prehension (inferior pincer)	7 months, 2 weeks	6 months - 10 months
Grasps, fine prehension (neat pincer)	9 months	7 months - 10 months

Source: In the Beginning, p. 320

WHY DOES MY BABY KICK OR HIT TOYS?

Kicking or hitting toys announces grabbing. Your baby clearly shows interest in the toy and tries to get to the object of interest using the whole body but doesn't quite succeed yet. During this phase, a baby gym is great to have, especially since your baby can achieve something just by hitting or kicking an object. The toys are attached and move up and down when the child touches them, so the child's efforts are rewarded!

WHAT CAN I DO TO HELP MY BABY LEARN HOW TO GRAB?

Whenever you notice that your baby wants to get a hold of something, hold the object of interest to where the baby can easily reach it. By observing carefully, you'll find out to what extent your child can manage the process of grabbing by his or her own efforts. You can help your child complete the process by, for example, turning the toy to where it fits better in his or her little hands. You'll realize that, over time, you'll have to help less and less.

WHY DOES THE BABY TAKE EVERYTHING APART AND THROW EVERYTHING ON THE FLOOR?

When we think of playing with building bricks, we mainly think of building a nice tower or stacking bricks. Your baby doesn't understand the concept of "creating" until accomplishing the leap of "programs." Before that, the child experiments with the individual parts and what can be done with them. That's why it's so fascinating for the child to knock over the tower you just built, to see everything fall down with a big racket, and to watch you skid across the floor collecting the pieces. The fascination for falling objects is so big because it goes right along with the leap of "events" at 19 weeks. The excitement over falling bricks is not destructive behavior, and it also doesn't mean that there's something wrong with your baby's fine motor skills, which are necessary to neatly stack bricks. As soon as your baby has accomplished the leap of "programs," he or she will enthusiastically build things and stack building bricks, which is good practice for fine motor skills. The baby will learn to move his or her hands in a way to put one brick on top of another.

WHICH TOYS ARE GOOD FOR PRACTICING FINE MOTOR SKILLS?

Basically, all toys with knobs or holes are suitable to practice fine motor skills. Puzzles, little bricks, or an activity center are ideal. However, toys aren't the only qualifying purchase; your child is also fascinated with household items. Give the little one a cup and a spoon to stir with, or ask your child to turn the pages of a book. Fine motor skills are so integrated in our everyday life that they can be practiced anywhere as long as it's fun. The main thing is how you practice them with your baby, not what you use to practice.

It's very important for you to demonstrate the movements clearly and calmly. For adults, it's nothing special to push a button, but it is hard work for your baby; the little one has to understand to use one finger instead of the whole hand and that the finger has to be moved precisely. If you demonstrate correctly, the child learns to master the skill a little quicker and better. Always demonstrate everything in a way that shows the baby exactly what's going on and how you use your hand. Praise the child's efforts even when he or she is not successful. Keep encouraging your child.

Keep in mind that the toy your baby plays with can't be too difficult to handle. For instance, try out the buttons of a toy before purchasing it. Some buttons are tight and hard to push. Choose a different one with buttons that can be operated easily. Some toys were made for babies but are not appropriate.

Chapter 3

SLEEP

Rest, Deep Sleep,
Sleep Patterns, Dreaming,
and Processing

During the first year, your baby goes through an enormous mental and physical development, making sleep essential. Unfortunately, it doesn't always come easy. Night after night, parents wander back and forth between their own bed and their baby's little bed in hopes of getting some shut-eye, if only for a few hours.

IS ENOUGH SLEEP IMPORTANT FOR THE BABY'S MENTAL DEVELOPMENT?

Your baby learns and discovers an abundance of new things, which is quite tough on the little one's body and brain. Of course, the brain, the organ where the mental development takes place, is part of the body, too. Besides food, the body also needs rest. With enough sleep, it's easier for your baby to learn new things and make new discoveries.

HOW DO I KNOW IF MY BABY IS GETTING ENOUGH SLEEP?

People are different, and this pertains to sleep as well. Not everybody needs the same amount of sleep; it depends on how much time our brain and nervous system need to recuperate. This rule applies to your child too, no matter the age. Of course, there are average values. While in the womb, the baby sleeps, on average, 23 hours per day. Shortly after birth, the baby sleeps an average of about 16 hours per day. The amount of sleep varies from 10 to 23 hours, though! A four-year-old child that goes to preschool sleeps about 12 hours, and also, some still take a nap of one to two hours.

DOES A GOOD MATTRESS INFLUENCE A BABY'S SLEEP?

A little baby seems to sleep soundly no matter where he or she is. However, you shouldn't skimp on a mattress, not because the little baby would sleep longer or fall asleep easier but because a good mattress provides support for the body and is much better for the baby's back, neck, and head. Once your baby is a little older, you'll realize that he or she will sleep better on a good mattress. It's easier for the body to relax, and the child remains in deep sleep longer.

WHY DOESN'T A BABY SLEEP WELL DURING A LEAP?

When a leap is about to happen, the baby's world is suddenly upside down. Without warning, everything looks different. The child is confused and bewildered, and you'll see it in the sleep pattern. Every baby reacts differently to a leap. One baby hardly sleeps, another sleeps less at night but more during the day, and another tries to go to sleep but sleep doesn't come.

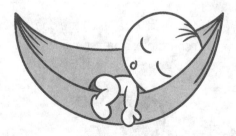

IS THERE SOMETHING I CAN DO TO MAKE MY BABY SLEEP WELL DURING A LEAP?

Unfortunately, there's no magic formula that could help you with getting your baby to sleep. Wouldn't that be nice? However, you can help by making sure that the baby can process the new impressions that come with a leap. Approach everything a little bit slower in the days around a leap. Postpone everything that's stressful and hectic, and be especially attentive to your child. You may have to reorganize your schedule somewhat, but in the long run, it means more calmness for your child and you.

HOW CAN I AVOID NOT GETTING ENOUGH SLEEP MYSELF AND BEING TOO EXHAUSTED TO BE A GOOD PARENT?

When your baby doesn't sleep well or not at all, you'll start to feel the consequences of a lack of deep sleep before too long. Some react more sensitively than others. Should you realize that you are too tired to pay proper attention to your baby (who needs you even more right now), you have to somehow make sure that you're getting your well-deserved rest. Just drop everything for a change, and allow yourself an hour of sleep while your baby is sleeping. Or ask your partner to take care of the child at night when the little one wakes up. If you are nursing, you can express breast milk in the evening.

IS THE DANGER OF SUFFOCATING OVER ONCE THE BABY IS ABLE TO TURN ON HIS OR HER SIDE AND PUSH UP WHEN LYING ON HIS OR HER STOMACH?

In the Netherlands, they advise to make the bed "short," which means use a sleeping bag according to the baby's body length instead of a big blanket to avoid the baby's face getting covered by the blanket and causing suffocation. At a first impression, the danger seems to be over once your baby is able to move sufficiently and turn over. This is deceiving, though. The baby's ability to turn from one side to another during the day doesn't necessarily mean that the little one is able to do this during the night while lying on a mattress. It's better to be on the safe side and keep using the sleeping bag.

WHY DOES MY BABY ALWAYS SLEEP WHEN WE HAVE COMPANY OR WHEN WE'RE VISITING?

Some babies aren't very comfortable in the company of many people. They close their eyes and fall asleep, or they "act" subconsciously as if they are sleeping much to the chagrin of many parents who would like to show off their little one's beautiful eyes and gorgeous smile. Nevertheless, it's not a good idea to wake your baby. Once your child is a little bit older, he or she will become more comfortable being around lots of people, and at that time, everyone will be able to see what a cute child you have.

SOMETIMES MY BABY BRIEFLY FALLS ASLEEP WHEN PLAYING—IS THIS NORMAL?

To the baby, anything new is tremendously exciting. Children are fascinated with everything they are able to do or learn to the extent of being completely engrossed in it and using up all their energy. Often, the child turns his or her head when a game is so exhausting that a short break is needed. That's a signal to you that your child needs a quick rest. Afterwards, the little one delves back into the game. This continues until you see the child's eyes turn away and the exhaustion gives way to a little nap, during which the child processes the latest experiences.

IS THERE A DIFFERENCE IN SLEEP BETWEEN BOYS AND GIRLS?

Studies have shown that, until the age of six months, boys need more sleep than girls. After that, it's the other way around; girls need more sleep than boys, and it'll stay that way for the rest of their lives. Once the children are a little bit older, girls are usually better at remembering their dreams than boys who dream just as often.

DO I HAVE TO BE COMPLETELY QUIET WHEN I WANT MY NEWBORN TO GO TO SLEEP?

You don't have to be as quiet as a mouse. When in your belly, the baby heard all the normal sounds in your surroundings and got used to them. If there's suddenly absolute silence, the baby may be missing something and stay awake or wake up because of the silence. Avoid noise but continue doing what you would normally do.

DO BABIES DREAM?

What goes on during a dream and why we dream remains a mystery. We do know, though, during which phase dreams happen. We don't dream during deep sleep but during the rapid eye movement (REM) phase. This phase has its name because the eyes move rapidly. It decreases during the first year after birth. Babies spend most of the night or day in the REM phase. A baby that is born after only 25 weeks of pregnancy spends the whole time sleeping in the REM phase. After 32 weeks, the REM phase covers 80 percent of sleep. Afterwards, the beginning of deep sleep starts to show. In children who are born close to their due date, sleep consists 45 to 65 percent of the REM phase. After three months, it's 43 percent; after 12 months, it's 30 percent, and once your child reaches puberty, it's only 20 percent.

Since the REM phases are longer in a baby, it seems to make sense that a baby dreams more than an adult. It's hard to tell whether babies' dreams are comparable to adults' dreams. Sometimes, you can tell your baby's dreaming. The question remains whether babies dream "stories" or whether they dream of principal feelings and emotions.

DO BABIES HAVE NIGHTMARES?

Starting with the leap of "relationships" (26 weeks or six months), many parents notice that their baby sleeps restlessly and moves a lot during sleep, which makes it look as if the baby is having a nightmare. Adults have nightmares every now and then, most times when under stress. Taking this into consideration, your baby may have nightmares more frequently when taking a leap.

SHOULD I WAKE MY BABY WHEN IT SEEMS LIKE HE OR SHE IS HAVING A NIGHTMARE?

Most times, a baby wakes on his or her own when having a nightmare. You don't have to wake your little one, but provide extensive comfort when he or she wakes up crying. For a baby, a nightmare is much scarier than it is for adults. We, adults, have the ability to compose ourselves when we wake up startled and realize that it was just a dream. Your baby is not capable of this. It's absolutely necessary that a trusted person provides the baby with comfort.

WHEN DOES THE BABY START HAVING A SLEEP PATTERN?

Sleep pattern means that the baby has a certain rhythm. This doesn't mean that the baby's rhythm coincides with yours. Before the baby was born, sleep-wake rhythm was already developed, which depended on Mom's sleep habits. Some babies adapt to the mother's rhythm, but normally, babies prefer the opposite. The little one becomes active when Mom wants to sleep and sleeps when Mom is running around, rocking the baby. As early as six months into pregnancy, babies have their own sleep-wake rhythm. This rhythm is as unique as a fingerprint. And your baby enters the world with this unique sleep-wake rhythm.

DURING WHICH LEAP IS THE DAY AND NIGHT RHYTHM DEVELOPING?

Even though there haven't been any studies regarding the connection between day and night rhythm and leaps in children, it is known that babies begin developing a day and night rhythm at the age of two to three months. You'll notice, though, that this rhythm is still a little bit off. Your baby starts sleeping through the night but doesn't fall asleep and wake up at the same times. Starting at the age of 15 weeks, you'll see more of a pattern. The day and night rhythm is also called circadian rhythm. You may support your child in finding the rhythm by making the difference in day and night very clear. During the night, it is dark. Thus, you shouldn't turn on a light when the baby's crying; go comfort or feed the little one. Talk to the baby in a quiet voice. By giving signals that mark the difference between day and night, it's easier for the child to develop a circadian rhythm.

WHY IS MY BABY'S BEDTIME GETTING PUSHED BACK MORE AND MORE?

You can't tell the sleep pattern of a newborn. This is perfectly normal. Once your baby has taken the first leap, you may start noticing the development of a certain sleep pattern. This rhythm is tuned in at 25 hours per day versus 24 because without outside signals, the human internal clock is programmed to 25 hours. That's the reason why your baby's sleeping hours during the day keep getting pushed back a little. During this phase, you'll also notice that the sleeping periods last somewhat longer and that your baby stays awake a little longer in between sleep phases.

The diagram below illustrates how a sleep pattern develops in a baby. A black line represents sleep, and a white line represents a waking state.

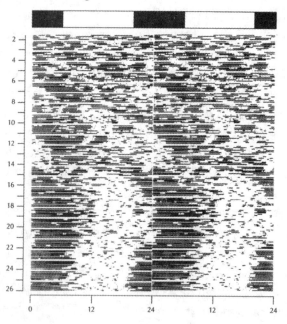

Source: N. Kleitmann & T.C. Engelmann (1953): Sleep characteristics of infants. In: Journal of Applied Physiology 6, S. 269 - 282

The black lines demonstrate how the sleeping periods keep getting pushed back a little bit.

The diagram also tells you that babies at the age of around 15 weeks have a steadier sleep pattern. So from that point on, you'll be able to better estimate when your baby will sleep.

WHEN WILL THE BABY START SLEEPING THROUGH THE NIGHT?

During the first months, 95 percent of all babies start crying when they wake up at night and need Mom or Dad. Sixty to 70 percent of all eight-month-old babies are able to fall back asleep on their own. Most parents are under the impression that their six-month-old baby sleeps through the night. Many development experts consider this "sleeping through the night" to be a milestone. This is not exactly true, though. Hardly any child under the age of 12 months sleeps through the night without interruption. Studies with hidden cameras have shown that babies do wake up but go back to sleep on their own. In fact, all children wake up one to three times during the night, usually starting after four hours of sleep.

AT WHAT AGE DO SLEEPING PROBLEMS START BECOMING RECOGNIZABLE?

You can't call it a sleeping issue until the baby is approximately six months old and should have a good day and night rhythm. Make notes of when and how often your baby sleeps. If you do this for a few weeks and you still think that your baby has problems sleeping, it would be best to contact your family practitioner or a consultation center.

MY BABY IS TOO ACTIVE TO GO TO SLEEP, ESPECIALLY AFTER A LEAP. WHAT CAN I DO TO HELP MY BABY FALL ASLEEP?

It's in some babies' nature to feel like they have to accomplish a new thing, and they don't want to quit trying. This behavior can already be observed at a very young age. The little ones don't stop until they have reached their goal. They demand a lot of themselves and you. This tenacity is a trait that will certainly help these children later in life, but sometimes, you have to protect the children from themselves. Emphasize on the trying of a new skill, and praise the attempts no matter the result. That way, you distract your child. If you notice that your child still demands too much of him- or herself, you need to interfere. Remove your child briefly from the situation and provide relaxing activities such as looking at a book together.

Five golden sleep tips

1. Provide a steady sleep ritual.
2. Avoid any kind of rush right before bedtime.
3. Make sure that the child's bed is in a room that's cozy and exudes serenity.
4. The room shouldn't be too warm or cold.
5. A relaxing bath or a massage before going to bed does wonders.

ARE THERE GUIDELINES FOR SLEEP RITUALS?

This is where your imagination comes in! Come up with your own fun and relaxing sleep rituals. Anything goes as long as it has a calming effect on your baby. Read a book to your baby, give the little one a bath, or rock him or her. There are lots of ways to calm down and relax your child. Agree with your partner on what you're going to do every evening, so both of you use the same ritual. A planned arrangement may seem very boring, but to your child, it's something to hold on to that helps him or her understand the situation of going to sleep. Make sure that you, too, are relaxed when putting the baby in bed. A child's antennae are much more sensitive than those of an adult. The child senses when you're stressed or in a hurry, so it's essential that you take enough time for the nightly sleep ritual. The serenity you radiate transfers to the baby, ensures that the baby goes to sleep quicker, and ensures that your baby sleeps through the night.

SHOULD THE CHILD HAVE A STUFFED ANIMAL IN THE BED?

A stuffed animal is cute and has a comforting effect, and the child can hold on to it. There's nothing wrong with it. However, don't force the stuffed animal on your child. If you put it in your child's bed every evening, you give your child the message that he or she can't go to sleep without it, and this is not the right message. Don't give your child the stuffed animal unless the little one asks for it.

DO BABIES GROW PHYSICALLY AND MENTALLY WHEN SLEEPING?

Sometimes, you get the feeling as if your baby grew overnight. There's something to it; although, this growth is not really measurable. During sleep, the growth hormone is produced in the hypophysis, which is an area in the brain that stimulates hormone production. The growth hormone is responsible for physical growth. Mental growth is not stimulated by this hormone. Mental development only takes place during leaps, and those take longer than just one night.

WHY IS MY BABY SUDDENLY SCARED WHEN I LEAVE THE ROOM EVEN THOUGH THIS WAS NOT THE CASE BEFORE?

Once your baby has accomplished the leap of "relationships" (around the age of six months), the little one suddenly realizes that you may walk away without him or her. The baby realizes that the situation (lying in bed) means that you're not with him or her and that it will last a while. Your baby is worried and shows it. The little one doesn't want you to leave anymore, which wasn't a problem before. The new fear is the result of the new understanding that was gained with the leap. Show your child that you understand the new situation. Simply sit for a little while with the child after putting him or her to bed, or go to another part of the room where the child can still see you. By respecting the fears and demonstrating that you're still there for him or her, the child's worries will vanish more quickly.

Chapter 4

CRYING

Calming Down,
Comforting, Processing,
and Communicating

All parents would prefer that their baby is laughing and happy all day long, but unfortunately, this is not always the case. Every baby cries, and all bewildered parents ask themselves why. They would like to comfort their baby and are searching for the right way to do this. When the baby is finally quiet after the parents have tried all kinds of things, they sigh in relief. It's all part of it.

WHY DOES A BABY CRY?

Your baby only has a few options to express him- or herself. The younger the baby, the more limited the options are. With every leap in development that the child accomplishes, he or she is better able to communicate with you both verbally and nonverbally. Until the child is able to really tell you what's wrong, you don't have a choice but to use his or her crying and body language as a guide. A crying baby is not sad, but crying signals that he or she is not feeling well for some reason.

THE MOST COMMON REASONS FOR CRYING ARE

○ Sickness or pain

○ Mental leap

○ Hunger

○ Frustration

○ Boredom

○ Lack of rest, cleanliness, or steadiness

○ Processing of the day

HOW DO YOU KNOW WHY THE BABY IS CRYING?

As parents, you quickly get to know your baby's various crying sounds. After only a few weeks together, you know what the baby wants when crying a certain way. However, sometimes, there are screaming fits that drive you to desperation because it hurts you to listen to your baby's crying when you absolutely cannot figure out the reason.

In this case, check the following:

○ Is the child sick (check for a fever), or could it be that the child is in pain? Pain is sometimes difficult to determine, especially in very young babies. Signals of pain include overly stretching of the body to one side or overly tightening or stretching of certain muscles. Pain due to intestinal cramps, for instance, is demonstrated by your baby's enormous stretching or pumping of the legs.

○ Whenever your baby takes a leap in mental development, the baby's world is upside down for quite a while. The little one is confused, so it's no wonder that there is more crying for longer periods of time during those days. Your baby may also cry differently than normal. Luckily, you can calculate the time of a leap; thus, you can easily figure out whether the crying is related to a leap.

○ The digestive system of a baby is completely different from ours, especially when the baby is still very little. Breast milk, for instance, is so easily digested that the baby is soon hungry again. This is one of the reasons why feeding on demand is much better than feeding according to a strict schedule. If a baby cries because of hunger, putting the baby to your breast quickly solves the problem. Formula is not as easily digested; therefore, babies are not hungry again soon after having a bottle. Satisfying your baby's hunger isn't difficult unless the baby doesn't suck hard enough when being breastfed or doesn't drink well when given a bottle (also see Chapter 5, "Diet," page 89).

○ Sometimes a little baby is simply frustrated. It's a misapprehension to think that more of an adult form of awareness is required in order to feel frustrated. Frustration means that there are conflicting interests or processes in the brain, causing the feeling of restlessness and tension. Your baby may, indeed, be frustrated because of not being able to get something across to you and because the baby doesn't know the reason for this feeling. You can take the frustration from your child with careful observation. Figure out what your baby likes and is interested in, and use it as a distraction. Since every baby is different, there are no hard-and-fast rules, but the more time you spend with your baby, the easier it gets. Interaction is even more important than time. The more you devote yourself to the child, the better you get to know him or her. If you sit for hours at a time next to your child's bed without saying or doing anything, you don't get to know your baby and you won't be able to find out the cause of frustration or how to distract the baby.

○ A baby can also be bored, no matter how little. There are extremely demanding babies and less demanding babies. The word "demanding" has a negative ring to it, but demanding babies usually have a distinct character and want to see, experience, hear, and feel lots of things. That's why a demanding baby requires more energy and action from you than a less demanding baby. If you give your child the stimulations, opportunities for experiences, and adequate attention, you'll notice that the child is less bored and cries less.

○ In the past, babies were raised on the basis of rest, cleanliness, and steadiness. Nowadays, we know that we shouldn't hang on too tightly to these rules. Exaggerated cleanliness, for example, isn't good for a child since the immune system becomes stronger by getting in touch with everyday bacteria. But there's also some truth in these rules. A baby is bothered by a dirty diaper and cries because of it. The other two rules, rest and steadiness, should not be neglected either. During the first year, your child learns, grows, and experiences more than during any year thereafter. The child takes in all the new impressions and is in dire need of rest. By providing a certain steadiness, you help your child deal with the various impressions. The chaos of going through leaps is enough for the little one already, so don't make it any worse. Create order by integrating routine throughout the day. This order brings calmness. Routine is important, not just for a baby but for all of us. During all the phases of development your child goes through, routine has a positive effect against whining and screaming fits, which you'll experience, no doubt about it (also see Chapter 9, "Parenting," page 147).

WHEN IS IT BABY COLIC?

If a baby cries more than three hours a day and more than three days a week over a time period of more than three weeks, it is called baby colic. Baby colic is an enormous burden for the parents. In order to find out whether you have a baby with colic, use the table on the next page as an aid. Write down how many hours and minutes your baby cries each part of the day and how long he or she sleeps. You may come to the conclusion that it just feels as if your baby is crying for hours, but it actually isn't all that bad once you really track the time and complete the table. This happens a lot. Crying is not fun for the child or for the parents, and that's why time seems to drag on.

If you've filled out the table for a week and your baby actually comes close to the hours of a colicky baby's crying, fill out the table for the following two weeks as well. If the crying behavior continues to where your baby is really colicky, contact your pediatrician or a consultation center.

WHAT IS A "WITCHING HOUR?"

A "witching hour" is the result of the maturation of the child's nervous system. The maturation enables the child to trade a short nap for longer periods of sleep. The maturation takes place in leaps, but these are not the same leaps as the leaps in mental development. The baby takes the first maturation leap at the age of around three to four weeks. Sleeping for three hours at a time does not happen until the age of 12 weeks, though. If the change in the sleep pattern causes your baby problems, it'll result in a "witching hour."

Monday	Night	Morning	Afternoon	Evening
Sleeps				
Is awake				
- Cries				
- Screams				

Tuesday	Night	Morning	Afternoon	Evening
Sleeps				
Is awake				
- Cries				
- Screams				

Wednesday	Night	Morning	Afternoon	Evening
Sleeps				
Is awake				
- Cries				
- Screams				

Thursday	Night	Morning	Afternoon	Evening
Sleeps				
Is awake				
- Cries				
- Screams				

Friday	Night	Morning	Afternoon	Evening
Sleeps				
Is awake				
- Cries				
- Screams				

Saturday	Night	Morning	Afternoon	Evening
Sleeps				
Is awake				
- Cries				
- Screams				

Sunday	Night	Morning	Afternoon	Evening
Sleeps				
Is awake				
- Cries				
- Screams				

DOES A "WITCHING HOUR" MEAN THAT THE BABY IS SAD?

The transition to a new sleep pattern is difficult (see Chapter 3, "Sleep," page 59). The child won't get over it until the age of 12 weeks. The baby's nervous system is still maturing. Until the nervous system matures, both deep sleep and light sleep aren't very effective. What goes wrong? During light sleep, you process what you've experienced during the day. Babies, too, do this in their own way. However, as long as the new rhythm hasn't quite worked out, the baby is unable to process everything that needs to processed, and that's the problem. During the first nap of the day, your baby processes a lot, but there's still some information that's left unprocessed. The same happens the next time the baby sleeps and the time thereafter. At the end of the day, lots of unprocessed experiences have accumulated. At the same time, sleep and wake periods become shorter throughout the day. Everything gets out of balance, and then comes the explosion: the "witching hour." As crazy as it may sound, the "witching hour" is liberating for your baby. It's Mother Nature's medicine to rebalance. By venting, your baby is finally able to process the accumulated impressions and emotions of the day. Now, the little one is ready for the next 24 hours.

WHEN ARE "WITCHING HOURS" MOST LIKELY TO OCCUR?

Between three and 12 weeks after birth, many little ones and their parents experience a daily "witching hour." They're most common when the baby is six weeks old. Often, parents are able to predict when it's about to happen because 85 percent of all babies are restless before it starts. The restlessness is an unmistakable signal for what's about to come. Usually, the crying stops after an hour or two, but sometimes, it may last four or even six hours. Luckily, there's some good news; once you've made it through the periods of crying, the baby usually sleeps longer and better and is better rested when awake.

WHAT'S THE BEST WAY TO COMFORT MY CRYING BABY?

Unfortunately, there are no tips on how to comfort with guaranteed success. It's usually the "classics" that work well. Your baby mainly wants rhythm, warmth, and safety. Walk around the room while rocking the baby in your arms. Sing or hum a song. Look at the child with a calm expression; try to make the best peaceful face you can, so your serenity will radiate to your child. The same applies to your voice. Say comforting words and use a soothing tone. Comfort the baby by saying that you understand and that you're there for the little one. A baby doesn't understand the words and their exact meaning but feels the intention of your words and is comforted.

IS IT POSSIBLE THAT MY REACTION TO MY BABY'S CRYING MAKES THE BABY EVEN MORE TROUBLED?

A baby reacts very sensitively to what parents feel and radiate. If your baby cries and you react as if you're annoyed, his or her crying will become even louder. Before you know it, it spirals down, and the crying lasts longer and longer. When in such a situation, you have to come to your senses. Forget everything around you for just a moment. Pay close attention to your aura. Breathe deeply and calmly, and let your child feel the calm breathing by laying him or her on your belly. The baby feels your belly evenly going up and down and gets calmer, too.

Sometimes, parents are unable to keep calm no matter how hard they try because the child's crying is too penetrating and long. They admit that they just can't take it any longer and can't bear to listen to their baby's screaming anymore. Don't feel guilty; we're all just human, and everybody has their limits. Never give up too fast, but don't push your limits, either. If the crying really starts to become too much, put your baby in bed for a little while and leave the room. That way, you avoid a fierce reaction to the baby's crying, which has more negative consequences than being alone for a short time.

AT WHAT POINT DO I NEED TO SEEK HELP WHEN MY BABY CRIES A LOT?

When it doubt, it's recommended that you contact a consultation center or the pediatrician, if only to relieve your worries. They may refer you to other aid organizations. Of course, this only happens if the situation calls for it. Many parents in this situation profit from "video-home training," which consists of videos that are taken at the parents' home that give them insights regarding the baby's crying behavior and the parents' reaction to it. Usually, it becomes clear to the parents what to do to make the situation more bearable.

WHY DO SOME BABIES GET QUIET WITH CERTAIN MUSIC?

Tests have shown that babies like music that sounds warm, full, round, and soft. When the rhythm of the music is slower than their heartbeat, babies calm down. Classical music works especially well. There are also special CDs that are composed in such a way that their sounds have a soothing effect on a baby.

WHY IS PHYSICAL CONTACT SO IMPORTANT WHEN COMFORTING A BABY?

You are the one who challenges the baby to get to know the world, and you are the one who gives the baby the feeling of emotional security while exploring the world. When you're close by, the baby feels safe. When the baby feels you, the feeling of emotional security is even stronger. The baby gets calmer and relaxes physically as well as mentally. It may be very difficult for you to hold your baby while he or she is screaming, but the feeling of helplessness makes the penetrating sound even worse. Try to stay calm and in physical contact with your child anyway. Don't forget that the situation is harder on your child than it is on you.

DOES A NEWBORN CALM DOWN BETTER WITH BODILY CONTACT?

Basically all babies love bodily contact. Some babies just show it more than others. The newborn loves to feel you close by. The warmth of your body, your heartbeat, and your voice remind the little one of the time in your womb. By the way, since the baby also knows Dad's voice from that time, he or she enjoys his attention as well. A baby sling is ideal for babies who like constant intimate contact. When using a sling, you always have the baby close to you, but at the same time, you have your hands free for other things. You may choose fabric that you can wrap or purchase a special sling. You can also use the sling as a hammock in the playpen. Go to a specialty shop for baby items and try out the various slings. Choose the sling that is comfortable and suits you the best.

IS IT NORMAL THAT MY BABY CALMS DOWN WHEN LYING ON MY NAKED BODY?

There's still kind of a taboo when it comes to nakedness. However, there's no reason to be embarrassed. Your baby loves to feel your naked skin against his or her body. That's why many babies get very calm when lying on Dad's or Mom's naked belly for a little while. They become so calm that they often fall asleep. When on your belly, the baby may fall asleep in the abdominal position. Always be considerate of safety when your baby's lying on your belly. For instance, never drink a hot drink, and never lay the baby naked on your belly when there's a draft.

IS MASSAGING A BABY A GOOD WAY TO COMFORT?

A baby massage is ideal for relaxing your child, and during the gentle massage, the baby becomes aware of his or her body. Therefore, a baby massage is far more than comfort or the promotion of relaxation. A baby that is uncomfortable for whatever reason will profit a lot from a relaxing massage.

Baby Massage

1. Put a little baby oil in your hands. Put your hands next to each other palms down so that both thumbs are set in the middle of your baby's chest. Using the palm of your hand, rub gently from the middle of the chest outwards. Repeat five times.

2. Now, it's the little arms' turn. Take one arm in both your hands close to the armpit. Then, massage one arm, working your way towards your child's little hand. Once your first hand is almost to the baby's hand, glide your other hand towards the baby's other hand. When the second hand is almost to the baby's hand, put your first hand close to the baby's armpit again. It may sound complicated, but it's not. If you do it right, you'll see that one hand is always massaging and that there is no interruption in the gentle rubbing movements.

3. You basically perform the same step again, but instead of the rubbing movement that goes straight to the baby's hand, make a spiraling motion.

4. Hold your baby's little hand in your hand, and using your thumb, massage the baby's palm. If you see that your baby really likes this, you may also massage the little fingers. Don't force anything, though. If your baby tightens his or her fist to where you can't open it, skip this step.

5. Repeat steps 2, 3, and 4 on the other arm. Make sure to keep contact between your baby and your hands when you switch over to the other arm. Massage with your fingers from one armpit across the chest to the other armpit.

6. Now, move your fingers across the chest and belly to the little legs. You do basically the same here as you did with the arms. Again, make sure you keep touching the baby when switching from one leg to the other.

7. Now, it's time to massage the little feet! Press one thumb on the heel and the other right before the toes and perform an up and down motion. Once your baby's a little older, he or she will start giggling.

8. Move back to the belly while keeping contact between your baby and your hands. Make circles with the palm of your hands that keep getting smaller the closer you get to the belly button.

9. Turn your baby on his or her stomach and perform long movements with your hands, starting at the neck and going across the back and down to the little feet.

The best thing to do is to make it a habit to massage your baby regularly, not only when the little one is going through a difficult time, because he or she loves it!

WHEN CAN I START MASSAGING MY BABY?

You can start massaging your baby as early as five weeks. Some experts say that it's ok from the fourth week on. Make sure that you don't massage your baby right after feeding; it's better to wait half an hour. Also, take in consideration your baby's general state. If the baby is very tired, you better wait until after a nap. Usually, right before the bath in the evening is the ideal time for the massage. During the bath, you can remove the massage oil with soap. Be careful when holding your child since your baby will be slick from the oil!

AT WHAT AGE DO TEARS APPEAR WHEN A BABY CRIES?

Your newborn doesn't cry tears yet. The first tears are not produced until the baby is about four months old.

Chapter 5

DIET

Intake of Food, Eating Behavior, Problems Eating and Drinking, and Impact of the Diet

You need energy to keep your body functioning. Your brain is, incidentally, the most energy-gulping organ! When your little one is two years old, he or she has more connections in the brain than at any point in his or her life, and the child's brain consumes twice as much energy as an adult's! The need for nutrition seems purely physical, but mental development also plays a role. If your baby does not feel well, he or she does not eat well, and if you breastfeed your baby, he or she not only drinks milk for the nutritional value but also enjoys it. If your toddler wants to become independent, he or she refuses your help holding a spoon. Nutrition is more than just taking in nutrients; it is a social event, a happening where the body and mind work together intensively.

DO I HAVE TO WRITE DOWN WHAT MY BABY TAKES IN EVERY DAY?

As long as your baby is growing well, you can assume that the child takes in enough nutrients. Within the first few days, it's important to see whether or not a newborn drinks well, so during this phase, you need to observe the little one extra carefully. When you leave the hospital after delivery, the pediatrician or clinic is in charge of continuing care. Your baby gets weighed, and you can monitor whether the child is growing accordingly. Unlike during your stay in the hospital, the child is not measured daily. It's not necessary anymore. From this point on, measurements are based on whether or not your baby is growing accordingly over a period of a few weeks, which also shows whether or not the baby has taken in enough nourishment.

DO I HAVE A REASON TO WORRY IF MY BABY SUDDENLY EATS OR DRINKS LESS?

Every now and then, your baby will have days during which he or she drinks less than usual. The smaller your baby is, the more you have to watch his or her drinking habits. When in doubt, you should visit a clinic or your pediatrician. Most times, it's probably a false alarm, but it'll ease your mind. It's perfectly normal that a baby drinks or eats less when not feeling well. You are not as hungry when you don't feel well, either. Your baby may start eating or drinking less shortly before the sickness starts. You'll also notice that eating behavior changes during a leap in mental development; the baby will likely eat less. This is part of a leap and is no reason for concern. Whenever you have doubts about your child's drinking or eating habits, ask your pediatrician.

MY BABY WANTS TO BE FED ALL THE TIME WHEN TAKING A LEAP IN DEVELOPMENT. DOES THE BABY NEED TO DRINK MORE DURING THAT TIME?

Fortunately, it is now known that it's better to breastfeed on demand, meaning you feed your baby when he or she wants to be fed. After all, your baby knows best if and when he or she is hungry. What makes breastfeeding sometimes a little problematic is that your baby doesn't just ask for your breast when hungry but also when trying to go to sleep or looking for comfort. Whenever your baby takes a leap, the familiar world is upside down, and the little one hangs on to what's familiar. What better way to hang on than to literally attach to Mom's breast? It may be very touching to you that your baby needs you so much. However, there's the danger of your nipples hurting when the baby sucks too hard or too long.

ARE PAINFUL NIPPLES ALWAYS A RESULT OF YOUR BABY SEEKING COMFORT BY SUCKING MORE FREQUENTLY?

It always depends on whether your nipples hurt just briefly or over a longer period of time. If your baby is visibly uncomfortable, such as during a leap, and demands your breast more often, there's no reason to worry. You don't need to change anything about the way you're feeding. If it becomes too much, you need to distinguish between feeding and comforting. Try to comfort your baby another way. Sometimes, it helps to warm the nipples shortly after feeding. You can do this with a blow dryer on the lowest setting. Also, let your nipples get some air as often as possible.

If sore nipples don't have anything to do with excessive sucking, there are usually three causes:

○ Your baby doesn't suck well enough.

○ The way you position the baby on your breast is not optimal.

○ You and your baby have thrush.

If your baby is not sucking well enough on your breast, it may be a result of sucking on a pacifier or bottle not made for breastfed babies. The baby needs a different sucking technique for these than for the breast, which leads to confusion. Therefore, in the beginning, you should refrain from using such products. Most often, your baby learns to suck properly on his or her own.

The right position is also very important because it makes it easier on your breasts. If you can't figure it out by experimenting, ask an expert at the clinic.

Thrush (Candida Albicans) is a fungal infection caused by yeasts and affects approximately four percent of all babies. You recognize the infection by seeing small white spots in your baby's mouth. Your nipples may be sore and hurting. Thrush is not dangerous but has to be treated. Visit your family practitioner if you suspect that your baby has thrush.

DOES MY BABY'S MENTAL DEVELOPMENT PROFIT IF I EAT LOTS OF FISH DURING PREGNANCY AND WHILE NURSING?

Every baby takes leaps in development at the same time and acquires the same perceptive abilities. What the baby uses the new ability for is mainly determined by hereditary factors. However, Harvard Medical School in Boston has proven that a diet rich in fish during pregnancy and nursing promotes a baby's mental development. The baby is better able to use the newly acquired perceptive ability. Please note that we're talking about fish that is low in mercury. The study also shows that high levels of mercury in the mother's blood have the opposite effect. Fish is healthy, so the positive impact on the baby's mental development makes sense.

DOES BOTTLE FEEDING VERSUS BREASTFEEDING HAVE AN IMPACT ON THE BABY'S MENTAL DEVELOPMENT?

Studies have shown that breastfeeding is preferable. Of course, it could be that you aren't able to nurse or decide against it. It doesn't have consequences for your baby's mental development. The baby takes the same leaps at the same set times, and as parents, you don't handle the leaps differently in breastfed babies than in bottle-fed babies.

AT WHAT LEAP CAN I START WITH SOLID FOOD?

You may start giving your baby solid food when he or she is between four and six months old. Of course, this is not a must. Some studies even disagree, saying that it's not recommended to give solid food this early. Various worldwide studies have shown that it's best to nurse a baby for six months before starting with solid food. If you don't breastfeed, give your baby formula until he or she is six months old. At this time, breast milk or formula is not enough anymore and giving solid food is a must. It doesn't have anything to do with a leap, but you probably shouldn't introduce the baby to his or her first spoon when the leap of "relationships" is about to happen. The baby takes this leap around 26 weeks after the calculated delivery date, which is about six months. During a leap, the little one isn't quite at ease. It's difficult enough for the child that his or her whole world changes, and the child really doesn't need to be introduced to anything new. You're better off introducing the child to solid foods either before or after the leap. Also, don't start solid foods when your baby is sick.

DOES A HEALTHY DIET HAVE AN IMPACT ON THE LEAPS IN DEVELOPMENT?

Eating well is always a good thing, especially when it comes to the mental development of your child, no matter the age. Your child takes the leaps at set times whether he or she is eating healthy or not. However, the new things the child is going to do or not going to do with the perceptive ability acquired during a leap is indirectly influenced by healthy food. An overweight child has to carry around more weight; thus, the child probably doesn't run as fast or as well. Also, any attempts the child takes to master new skills require the brain to play along. As is generally known, the whole body works better when it's healthy and gets all the important nutrients.

DOES DRINKING JUICE OR WATER HAVE AN INFLUENCE ON MENTAL DEVELOPMENT?

Once you start feeding solids at the age of six months, you'll probably let your baby drink from a sippy cup every now and then. Get the child used to a normal cup as soon as possible before the age of nine months. Not only is this much better for his or her teeth but it also promotes the development of chewing and speech. By providing optimal conditions for your child to learn how to talk, you help the little one with mastering this skill to the best of his or her ability.

IF MY FIVE-MONTH-OLD BABY SUDDENLY PUTS EVERYTHING IN HIS OR HER MOUTH, IS IT A SIGN THAT I NEED TO FEED SOLIDS?

As soon as your baby has completed the leap of "events" (19 weeks after the calculated delivery date or four and a half months), you'll see that the baby puts things in his or her mouth more often, including your fingers, toys, and items lying around; everything is interesting to your baby and fun to put in his or her mouth. However, this doesn't mean that your baby is hungry but is a logical consequence of this leap. The baby investigates objects by feeling them with his or her lips and putting them in his or her mouth. You have to really pay attention to what the little one investigates! When the baby puts things in his or her mouth that are dangerous, you need to warn him or her by saying "Ouch!" or "No!" Take the object from the baby and explain why you're doing it. The baby won't exactly understand what you're talking about but learns that there are certain things that cannot be put in his or her mouth.

AT WHAT AGE DOES A BABY SHOW THAT HE OR SHE IS HUNGRY OR FULL?

Starting on day one, you recognize if your baby's hungry or has had enough to eat by using your intuition. Once you get to know your baby better, you quickly figure out which kind of crying means what. As soon as your baby has taken the leap of "events" (19 weeks after the calculated delivery date or four and a half months), the child will demonstrate hunger in a different way. The baby will reach for your food or drinks and make smacking sounds when wanting to be breastfed or when seeing the bottle. Many parents know their little one is full if the baby spits out the food or pushes the breast or bottle away. The baby suddenly seems much more mature.

AT WHAT AGE DOES A BABY START HAVING FOOD PREFERENCES?

As long as the baby is younger than six months old, he or she likes pretty much anything and doesn't have any preferences. Once your baby has taken the leap of "relationships" (26 weeks after the calculated delivery date or six months), you'll realize that your baby likes some foods better than others. Of course, this is great since it shows that your child is developing; food preferences represent a milestone as well. But all the fun is over when the preferences get to where the daily eating rituals turn into torture. A strong-willed child doesn't just let you know of preferences but simply refuses food that isn't liked. As parents, you'll start having doubts whether you're really feeding your child well since you know that a variety is extremely important when it comes to eating healthy. However, make sure that this milestone doesn't become a constant issue. It doesn't do any good at all to make your child eat or to force healthy foods on the little one.

WHAT CAN I DO IF MY CHILD REFUSES FOOD?

Luckily, it hardly ever happens that foods and sometimes even liquids are refused to the point of malnourishment or dehydration. If you are worried that this is the case with your baby, contact your pediatrician immediately. Most often, it's a completely different and harmless kind of food denial. For example, your child may deny the food because he or she prefers something else, thinks it's funny that you're following him or her with the spoon, or doesn't have an appetite because he or she is constantly being offered food by Mom or Dad. Therefore, never force your child to eat. If your child doesn't want to eat, set the food aside and offer it again a little later. Don't turn meals into a power game because your child will last longer than you.

Also, keep in mind that it is solid food we are talking about. Of course, solids contain nourishment, but their main purpose in the beginning is to get your baby used to different flavors and used to chewing and swallowing.

As soon as solids become a primary source of nutrients, you may expect more of the little one when it comes to eating. At that point, you'll make the decision when it comes to food, and you'll give your child a chance to signal you when he or she is full. If the child refuses the food but really didn't eat enough, the little one doesn't get dessert or a snack until having cleaned his or her plate. That way, you'll clearly bring the message across to your child that there will only be dessert after the main course has been eaten.

WHEN DOES A CHILD START BEING ABLE TO EAT BY HIM- OR HERSELF?

Once your child has taken the leap of "sequences" (46 weeks after the calculated delivery date or 11 months), the little one understands that some things have to be done in a certain sequence in order to reach a certain goal. Given that your baby finds this skill interesting, you may see your child take a spoonful of food and move it towards his or her mouth while he or she is processing the leap. These are the first signs of independent eating. Of course, you can't expect your baby to eat every meal on his or her own from now on. Give the baby the opportunity to try it over and over again even though it creates a big mess. If you notice that your little one gets tired or impatient, take the spoon and feed him or her the rest of the meal. Of course, you need to praise your child for how well he or she is eating on his or her own.

IS IT IMPORTANT TO LET MY CHILD EAT ON HIS OR HER OWN?

It's always important to support your child's independency and the efforts given while learning something new. This pertains to eating and drinking as well. At some point, your baby will show you that it is important to him or her to do these things without your help. With every leap in development that your child takes, "do-it-yourself" becomes increasingly important. Once the child has completed the leap of "sequences," "do-it-yourself" gets to be a big deal. At that point, children want to eat by themselves when sitting at the dinner table. Some parents may lose their patience when they see that more food ends up on the floor than in the child's mouth, or they suffer because the child really wants to eat without help but is completely frustrated because it doesn't work the way it's supposed to. Try to help your child in a positive way. Praise the efforts, or make a game of it. Take a spoon in your hand, and give another one to your baby. Your baby feeds you, and you feed your baby. That way, the little one feels "big," and you're making sure that the baby still gets enough to eat.

WHEN DO I NEED TO START PAYING SPECIAL ATTENTION TO HEALTHY FOOD?

Eating healthy is always important for mother and child, starting at pregnancy. You're not allowed to eat certain foods anymore because they're harmful to the baby. Once your child is allowed to snack, you really have to pay attention to healthy food since the child will try to get his or her hands on yummy stuff and disregard "normal" food. So make it a habit from day one to pay attention to healthy food. Good nourishment pays off throughout life. By teaching your child early on, you'll help your child avoid health issues, including obesity and diabetes, later in life. Rule by example: consciously eat healthy!

BESIDES NUTRIENTS, WHAT ELSE DO I HAVE TO PAY ATTENTION TO WHEN IT COMES TO EATING AND DRINKING?

Good nourishment supplies the body with all the important nutrients. However, eating and drinking is more than just taking in nutrients; it's also a social phenomenon. Make sure that the whole family eats together at the table. Once your child is old enough, ask for help with anything pertaining to meals from grocery shopping to doing the dishes. By helping, the child not only gets the opportunity to take on some responsibility within the family but also subconsciously learns good eating habits. You can even teach your toddler to treat food sensibly in a playful way. Especially after the leap of "programs" (55 weeks after the calculated delivery date or 13 months), the child will be excited about the activities on the next page and will be happy to help. The child won't really understand some of the games until the leap of "principles" has been completed (64 weeks after the calculated delivery date or 15 months).

- ○ Ask your child to help you take groceries from the shelves and put them in the shopping cart.
- ○ Ask your child to help you put away the groceries at home.
- ○ Ask your child to put his or her plate and silverware on the table. Children who learned to walk early may be able to do this on their own. If your child is not walking or standing safely yet, he or she can help while sitting in the highchair. Give the child his or her plate, and ask the little one to put it on the table or the tray of the highchair.
- ○ Ask your child to stir something for you.
- ○ While you're cooking, give the child a few food items, a bowl with water, and a spoon. That way, the little one can "cook" something, too. Help him or her if you need to. Of course, you need to try it and say how delicious it is!
- ○ Ask your child to help with the dishes. It's going to be lots of splashing but guaranteed fun for the both of you!

Chapter 6

EMOTIONAL DEVELOPMENT

Secure Attachment Bonds,
Fear of Strangers, Separation
Anxiety, Experiences and
Feelings, and Self-Confidence

Intelligence alone doesn't make you happy. The way someone is set in life, the joy he or she has in life, and the self-confidence he or she has are all aspects that determine a pleasant or less pleasant life. Therefore, your baby's emotional development is not less important than his or her physical development. Provide a good start in life by being very conscious of your baby's emotional development.

WHEN DOES A CHILD'S EMOTIONAL DEVELOPMENT START?

Although we know a lot about unborn babies, it's still difficult to analyze the feelings of a baby in the womb. However, researchers are becoming more and more knowledgeable on the subject. Feelings are connected to the production of hormones, and this is already happening in the womb. Therefore, feelings can be measured physically. Fright reactions are the visible results of feelings. Considering this, you can see and feel that a baby has feelings in the mother's womb already. For instance, if there's a sudden, loud noise close to you, your baby reacts with a severe turning movement or a kick. Some babies are even startled by an echo and hide their heads behind the pubic bone.

DOES A NEWBORN BABY ALREADY FEEL SOMETHING LIKE HAPPINESS, SADNESS, AND PLEASURE?

The newborn experiences the world as something like "soup." Everything the little one perceives, sees, smells, tastes, or hears is one comprehensive experience, one big entity. The baby experiences it in this way until the leap of "sensations" (five weeks after the calculated delivery date). Therefore, the newborn doesn't only hear a loud noise but senses this unpleasant feeling with his or her whole body. All of a sudden, the baby is uncomfortable. The newborn also reacts with his or her whole body when it comes to pleasant things as well. Roughly speaking, the baby experiences everything as positive, negative, or neutral. The older the baby gets and the more leaps in development the baby goes through, the more the baby is able to distinguish feelings. A positive feeling can then be perceived as happiness, pleasure, love, etc. However, this doesn't mean that your newborn has fewer feelings and that you need to be less considerate of them. It's quite the opposite, especially since the baby isn't able to divide the feelings into different emotions; the baby's reactions are more severe now than they are later.

WHAT ARE SECURE ATTACHMENT BONDS?

The expression already says it: to feel secure in relationships. To your baby, it refers to the relationship with you first and foremost. The little one needs this secure bond. Babies want to feel your unconditional love and know that you are always there for them because of who they are, not what they are able to do or not do. For a newborn, this "feeling" is still natural. As long as there is skin contact, preferably belly to belly, and the baby hears your loving voice, everything's soon okay again. Once the child becomes mobile and starts to go on excursions (from the secure base, which is you, of course), it's important that you are predictable, present, and available. The child has to be able to trust that you're still there when he or she returns from excursions. These excursions are very short at first and are often within your arm's reach. If you get up and walk away, the child becomes insecure and may hang on to you. To be on the safe side, avoid suddenly walking away. During this phase, you often see babies whining and crawling after their parents or crying for their parents if they aren't able to crawl yet. The older your baby gets, the more complex the interactions between you and your child become. These interactions play a role in secure attachment bonds.

HOW DO SECURE ATTACHMENT BONDS DEVELOP?

Secure attachment bonds don't come naturally; they develop over time. They can't be scheduled in your planner. You allow your baby to feel secure attachment bonds in everything you relay to your baby. The important thing is that you respect your baby's dignity and fulfill his or her needs in a loving manner. In the beginning, these needs are purely physical; later, they are more complex and are predominately mental needs.

HOW DO I RESPECT MY CHILD'S DIGNITY?

No mother or father would likely hurt their child's dignity on purpose. If parents make mistakes here, it's not on purpose but occurs most often unknowingly. To avoid mistakes, you should always be aware of which step in mental development your baby is on. By thoroughly reading up on leaps in development, you'll get an increasingly better insight into your child's world and know what is understood and what isn't. If you take this into consideration, you'll find the key to your child's unique personality and respect his or her dignity.

HOW DO I FULFILL MY CHILD'S NEEDS IN A LOVING WAY?

The difficult thing about parenting is not the precise fulfillment of a child's needs but discovering what the needs are in the first place. If a child is whiny because he or she is not allowed to touch something, touching it seems to be the child's need. Your child probably thinks that this is the greatest need right now. However, the real need is the need to learn rules. To fulfill your child's needs doesn't mean that you have to go by what your child wants at all time.

WHAT ARE THE PRIMARY EMOTIONAL NEEDS OF EVERY BABY?

Starting on day one, a baby is busy with self-development and finding a place in society in a very primitive and subconscious way. However, the expressions, "self-development" and "finding a place in society" deflect many primary emotional needs.

HOW DO I BRING MY CHILD'S NEEDS IN ACCORDANCE WITH MY OWN?

In general, you'll realize that, with some dexterity, you'll satisfy both your and your child's needs. Secure attachment bonds don't mean that your child rules over all the other family members. The child needs to learn that Mom and Dad are sometimes busy with other things, and therefore, the little one may have to wait now and then. A child understands this after the leap of "programs," which is at the age of about one year (also see Chapter 9, "Parenting," page 147).

Primary emotional needs for a child during "self-development:"

○ Being exposed to games and situations pertaining to the things the child is fascinated with during a leap

○ Parents who understand what their child is fascinated with and why something is interesting

○ Parents who are there for their child when they're needed

○ Parents who respect their child's dignity

○ Parents who put the child's interests first

○ The feeling that the child is love because of who he or she is, not what he or she does or is unable to do

○ Realizing that the child is allowed to have feelings; the child is allowed to be sad or afraid when startled

○ Parents who take his or her feelings seriously and are there for him or her

○ Knowing where the child stands

○ Feeling that the child is part of a bigger entity, a family

○ Being allowed to be him- or herself

These are, by far, not all of your child's primary needs. Secure attachment bonds can't be put into a list of ingredients with the end result being a perfect recipe. Secure attachment bonds form over the duration of one's life and don't really ever have an unchangeable end result.

HOW DO I HANDLE MY CHILD'S UNPLEASANT EXPERIENCES?

Every child experiences situations that aren't pleasant or are even hurtful, both physically and emotionally. Of course, you try to avoid these situations as much as you can, but sometimes, they simply can't be prevented. For example, vaccinations are necessary for your child's health. Your child doesn't like being poked by the needle and doesn't understand why this has to happen. Some parents say that their child still looks at them hours after the vaccination as if wanting to say, "You traitor." You then ask yourself whether the vaccination is at odds with secure attachment bonds. A vaccination is just one example, of course, and there are numerous other unpleasant situations that you don't have any control over. In this case, you have to tell yourself that these experiences may be unpleasant for the little one but are best for the child in the long run.

By accepting that you can't spare your child those experiences, you'll avoid panicking yourself and doubting your abilities as parents. Try to see the positive side. You can prove to your child that you are reliable and as solid as a rock, especially during times of sadness and pain. Be considerate of your child's feelings and provide comfort. Calm your child with your voice and show empathy. Tell your child that you understand that it hurts and is unpleasant. Let the little one cry about the pain, but be reassuring and say that the pain will go away.

IS THERE A CONNECTION BETWEEN SAFE SECURITY BONDS AND THE COMPLETION OF A LEAP IN MENTAL DEVELOPMENT?

The older your child gets, the longer the leap becomes and the longer the bewilderment lasts. During this time, your child is especially clingy, whiny, and moody. The child cries a lot and always wants to be near you. The leap turns the familiar world upside down, so the child hangs on to you as the familiar person. Of course, this is more pronounced in some babies than in others, but for the parents, it remains a difficult and sometimes frustrating period of time. It's best to provide secure attachment bonds by first understanding that the confusion is not the baby's fault. Your baby is under an enormous amount of stress when taking a leap; thus, the child literally screams for the feeling of safety and comfort from you during this difficult phase.

WHAT CAN I DO IF MY CHILD GETS ON MY NERVES TOO MUCH OR IF I'M SO TIRED THAT IT'S DIFFICULT FOR ME TO SHOW UNCONDITIONAL LOVE?

The difficult phase of a leap also takes its toll on the parents, and some parents realize that they're reaching the limit of what they can endure. All of a sudden, you slap your child, which is against all beliefs. If it came to this, you really went too far, and you took it out on your child. You hurt the child's dignity, which doesn't promote positive secure attachment bonds. Your child depends on you, and you have to be reasonable.

It's not a shame to realize your own limits. It's actually the opposite; it's good and will contribute to secure attachment bonds. Take precautions when it's really getting to be too much for you. Ask someone to watch your baby for a few hours while you go for a walk or take a nap. Make sure that your batteries get fully recharged, so you can commit to giving your child loving care again.

WHAT DOES FEAR OF STRANGERS AND SEPARATION ANXIETY MEAN?

Once the baby has taken the leap of "relationships" (around six months of age), many parents notice that the child suddenly isn't quite comfortable in the presence of strangers anymore. The child seems to be afraid of them and hangs on to the person that he or she is most comfortable with. The term "strangers" is used in the widest sense of the word. One baby is skittish with the neighbor who knows the baby while another is only skittish with people whom he or she has never met. The fear of strangers may vary between six months and one year, and for some children, it lasts until the age of two years. The child's fear of other people is often connected with the fear of being separated from the person that the child relates most closely with, which is you, of course. Suddenly, your baby is afraid when you leave the room or even move to another area of the room. It's because the child now understands the loss of control in regards to being close to you. This fear is called separation anxiety.

WHAT CAN I DO ABOUT MY CHILD'S SEPARATION ANXIETY?

Help your baby understand that even though you're out of sight sometimes, you're still there for him or her. For instance, keep talking when you leave the room, so the baby hears your voice and knows that you're still there even if the little one can't see you anymore. You can also use games to teach your baby that something is still there even if it's not visible. For example, put a towel over a toy, and ask your baby, "Where's the toy?" Then, pull the towel from the toy, and in a happy voice, say, "There's the toy!" Your baby will like this little game, especially after completing the leap of "relationships." These simple hiding games have endless options for variety.

HOW CAN I HELP MY BABY GET THROUGH THE SKITTISH PHASE?

First of all, you have to understand that the fear of strangers is perfectly normal, and it's important to not dismiss the child's fears as nonsense. However, you don't need to spare your baby during this phase by avoiding strangers as much as possible. Keep inviting people you would normally invite, and visit them if you feel like it. Ask your visitors or hosts to leave your baby alone at first. Keep your baby in your lap for a little while, and let the baby decide at what point he or she wants to approach others or gradually leave the safe spot of Dad's or Mom's lap to sit somewhere else or to crawl around. Always let the baby take the lead. The little one gets to decide when others may approach him or her. That way, you're giving the child a chance to overcome the fear on his or her own, which is a good investment for further development. In the short run, you reduce the time of skittishness and make it easier to deal with, and in the long run, you help your child become self-confident.

CAN I TAKE MY CHILD TO A DAY CARE CENTER IF THE CHILD IS AFRAID OF STRANGERS?

If your child is very skittish right now, it's not the best time to improve his or her independency. It's better to get your child used to a babysitter or day care center either before or after this phase.

Also, keep in mind that babies that are already going to a day care center and are used to it may suddenly not want to go there anymore or may become afraid of the caretaker. Talk to your babysitter or caretaker about your child's current skittishness. Ask the person to cuddle with your child or leave him or her alone when you're leaving. Whether the caretaker cuddles your baby or leaves him or her alone depends on the child's preferences, and you're only able to find out by testing different scenarios. You may want to call the babysitter or caretaker half an hour after you leave and ask how your child is doing. At least, this will appease you.

WHAT SHOULD I DO WHEN MY CHILD IS AFRAID OF STRANGERS AND WANTS TO ONLY BE WITH ME, BUT I REALLY HAVE TO LEAVE FOR A MOMENT?

At some point, your child will experience that you have to leave for a little while without them. Every child will eventually have a problem with this and will make it quite clear to you that he or she does not agree with the situation. Here are some tips to make the parting easier for your child:

○ Tell your child in clear, understandable words that you have to leave for a little while but that you'll be right back. You may also say where you're going. Be brief and don't turn it into a long story; otherwise, you'll create doubt in your child.

○ Give your child a big kiss, say goodbye, and leave. If you let your child upset you with his or her crying or other forms of protest, your child will notice, which makes saying goodbye even more difficult.

○ Never sneak off. By doing that, your child will learn that you may suddenly disappear if the little one doesn't always keep an eye on you, worsening separation anxiety.

CAN YOU TEACH TODDLERS SELF-CONFIDENCE?

Self-confidence is something a toddler may experience to some extent around the age of one to two years, but it isn't consciously experienced until the child is older. Self-confidence is really a feeling. However, you may set the foundation for this feeling from the cradle on by supporting your baby during development. Expose your baby to various situations that require your baby's effort. Let the baby try out things that are possible yet challenging at the same time and that are difficult but never too difficult. That way, your baby learns early on that he or she can do things when he or she puts forth the effort. Your assistance lies in creating surroundings that provide your child with a chance to be successful in his or her efforts. For instance, you may put a toy where the baby can easily reach it and practice grabbing. You may keep the distance between you and another person so short that the baby is able to walk from one person to the other in just two steps. This gives the baby the feeling of actually having walked a short distance all on his or her own, making the little one and you, of course, tremendously proud! You need to show how proud you are by extensively praising and encouraging your child in a happy voice, but you must also praise your baby even if something doesn't work out. In this case, you're simply proud of your little sweetie's efforts. Children and their self-confidence grow with encouragement, success, and praise!

WHY IS SELF-CONFIDENCE SO IMPORTANT? AND WHY DO YOU HAVE TO START WITH IT WHEN THE CHILD IS STILL A TODDLER?

Self-confidence is one of the most important requirements for creating a successful and secure life. Self-confidence goes hand-in-hand with self-knowledge and the knowledge of one's own limits. A girl with self-confidence won't easily get into a perilous situation. A boy with self-confidence won't easily be convinced to participate in stupid and dangerous activities. People who were "fed" self-confidence early on know and are able to set their limits later in life.

HOW DO I ACT TOWARDS MY CHILD WHEN THERE'S STRESS AT HOME?

Babies have very fine antennae regarding the atmosphere at home and within the family, and sometimes, there may be stress, including trouble at work, illness of a family member, or a break-in. There are lots of worries and problems we don't have any influence on. Sometimes, it may cause a stressful day for the parents, but sometimes, the period of stress may last longer, as is the case with grief, for instance. You are not your usual self and don't feel well, and your baby senses it. You can't avoid these kinds of situations, but you can make them as bearable as possible for everyone. First of all, accept that the situation is what it is. It doesn't do any good to hide your feelings. Deliberately plan for more calmness in your daily routine, especially within the areas you have influence on.

Chapter 7

STRESS

Problems and Disagreements
in Parenting, Doubts,
Overextension, and Stress
Reduction

Having a baby is one of the most beautiful experiences in life and leads to the biggest changes in life. Nothing is the way it was before. Planning your daily routine, your values in life, and your level of energy all change; everything changes. In short, you see the world with different eyes, which sometimes brings great tension to you and your family. The tension shows itself in moments of despair, during times of emotional distress, and during arguments or alienation between you and your partner, your other children, your parents, or your in-laws. These are unpleasant moments of parenthood, but they are part of it and perfectly normal.

IS IT NORMAL THAT I'M SOMETIMES DOWNRIGHT DESPERATE AS A PARENT?

Sometimes, your baby may ask a lot of you during the difficult phase of a leap in development. The baby doesn't do this on purpose but does so instinctively. The child's whole world is upside down, and there's confusion. Therefore, the little one resorts to the one pillar, Mom and/or Dad. The child literally hangs on to you. Although you know that you have to be there for the child, you often react as if you're annoyed, and sometimes, you're overcome by a feeling of helplessness. It's still a taboo for many parents to admit this, and they have other parents' statements on their minds saying they never have any problems with it. The fact is, of course, that most mothers and fathers know these feelings quite well. Whenever the baby takes a leap, your patience is put to a severe test. You're just a human being, so accept that you're pretty desperate every now and then. Discuss your feelings with your partner. Don't take your frustration out on your baby! Admitting to feelings of despair and accepting and talking about them proves that you're a good parent. You'll realize that this eases the stress and makes it easier on your baby and your whole family.

HOW CAN I AVOID BEING STRESSED WHEN MY CHILD IS ABOUT TO GO THROUGH A LEAP?

First and foremost, you have to accept the fact that leaps are part of a baby's development and that these phases are not pleasant for your baby; therefore, they have an effect on you, your partner, and your other children. You can prepare for a leap if you know what's going on in your baby's little head and what the little one is up against. Preparing yourself for the leaps shortens the difficult time and reduces the stress for you, your baby, and your whole family.

WHAT CAN I DO IF IT SEEMS LIKE EVERYTHING IS GETTING TO BE TOO MUCH FOR ME?

Parenthood demands a lot of you, mentally and physically. Whenever your baby is going through a leap, you may get the feeling every now and then that the limit is reached, and sometimes, it's the last straw that breaks the camel's back. Some parents have tears of despair and exhaustion in their eyes. You get to a point where you realize that everything is getting to be too much; it's not about a stressful moment during which you're briefly fed up and back to laughing in five minutes. It's very important that you are able to distinguish between a touch of resignation and true emotional distress. A moment of despair is often solved by a good cry in the arms of your comforting partner. A longer and more severe low is not overcome as easily or quickly, of course. If possible, try to not let it get to that point. Don't only have your baby's well-being in mind but your own as well. Make it clear to yourself that your health is also important for your child's well-being. After all, a happy Mom and Dad are able to pass on more happiness to their child than unhappy parents. Recognize your limits, and don't be afraid to tell your partner or your doctor when you have reached your limit.

HOW DO YOU AVOID TRUE MENTAL DISTRESS?

Some people may be more sensitive to stress than others, and some get to the point of mental distress a little easier than others. The reason for the difference doesn't really matter much here. It's about how you prevent getting into mental distress or getting depressed for your own interest, your child's interest, and your family's interest. It's important to recognize the symptoms early on. If you realize that a mental low is about to happen, you need to raise alarm immediately. Come up with a plan to get out of the stress spiral. Ask your partner for more help with the baby, and make note of those days on your calendar. Do something fun during those times. Go for a walk, go swimming, or indulge in shopping. Don't feel guilty in the least about taking those time-outs. By being considerate of yourself, you avoid getting into severe mental distress and not being able to fulfill your baby's needs. Don't shy away from discussing depression with your family practitioner or someone at a consultation center.

IS IT BAD IF MY BABY SEES ME CRYING?

Your baby senses how you're feeling if you're sad and if you're crying. In the beginning, the baby literally even tastes your feelings through the breast milk, so it's not about the tears that are flowing but the feeling that comes with them. Your baby would rather see you happy and cheerful because then he or she is happy and cheerful, too. This doesn't mean that you absolutely aren't allowed to cry in your baby's presence, but every now and then, you just have to pull yourself together. Whenever you are sad, it's a good idea to let your baby know that it's not because of him or her. Cuddle with the little one, smile, and try to replace your tears with feelings of happiness as quickly as you can.

HOW DO YOU COME TO KNOW YOURSELF AND YOUR PARTNER AS A NEW COUPLE AFTER A BABY IS BORN?

Up until the birth of your child, you knew each other solely as a man and a woman who have been together for a quite some time. This changes completely the moment you have a baby. You now have something unique together and share responsibility. Never before have you experienced responsibility to this extent. You are deeply touched by your baby, and you realize that your partner feels the same. Men, who usually throw their weight around, walk around for days with tears of joy in their eyes, and the most self-confident women may suddenly have doubts with every diaper they change. It seems as if you were born again when your baby was born. A woman is born a mother and a man a father. Often, you realize a few months after birth that you've gotten pretty used to the new role.

HOW DO YOU HANDLE DISAGREEMENTS REGARDING THE BABY'S CARE DURING THE FIRST FEW MONTHS?

Since there are so many new things ahead that you both don't have any experience with, it's completely normal that you are searching for a while to find the right approach to handling your offspring. During the first few months after birth, the focus is often on how to establish your new life effectively. Many disagreements are about sleeping, crying, feeding, and experimenting with the leaps in mental development. You have to look for strategies that are acceptable to you as well as your partner. Love and comfort are amongst the elementary things to give to your baby, and you have to rule by example. Two stressed out and constantly fighting parents have never contributed to a relaxed atmosphere at home.

Communication, as banal as it may sound, is the only thing that really helps you two get on the same page. While the baby is sleeping, agree to talk about everything and take your time when doing so. Be understanding of your partner's opinions because both of you want the best for your baby.

IS IT NORMAL THAT MY PARTNER AND I ARGUE MORE OFTEN WHEN OUR BABY IS GOING THROUGH A LEAP?

If your baby cries a lot or doesn't sleep or feel well, it takes a toll on the whole family. A leap is tough on your baby; thus, the baby is difficult. As a parent, you're bewildered, thinking something may be wrong. Your sleep is interrupted because the baby wakes up a lot. After a few days filled with worries and little sleep, your stress level has reached its limit. So the leap in mental development doesn't only result in your baby going through a difficult phase, but it's also a tough time for you. The spiral keeps going. When Mom or Dad is stressed, it naturally has an impact on the whole family. Of course, this doesn't improve the atmosphere at home, which the baby who's already very sensitive senses. The baby then becomes even more "difficult." You see, a leap has far-reaching consequences!

WHAT DO I DO IF MY PARTNER AND I WANT TO HANDLE A DIFFICULT PHASE FOR OUR BABY IN DIFFERENT WAYS?

No doubt, it's always better when Dad and Mom agree, especially during difficult times. When your baby is going through a leap and is flustered all day long, doesn't eat well, cries a lot, and doesn't sleep much, it leads to testiness in both of you before long. Unlike other decisions you have to agree on, a leap is something that comes and goes, so keep this in mind when discussing how to proceed. You can plan ahead and determine how you want to handle the situation and distribute the responsibilities together. The questions on pages 125 and 126 may be helpful in drawing up an appropriate plan. There's not a right or wrong answer; the answer you agree on is the right one.

HOW DO YOU FIND TIME FOR ONE ANOTHER WITH ALL THE STRESS OF THE BABY?

The time you spend alone together is clearly less than it was before the baby was born, and this is putting it mildly. Going to the movies on a whim is out of the question. If you want to be alone together, you have to do so while your baby's asleep or hire a babysitter. In the beginning, this takes some getting used to. Most often, it's not the women that have a problem with it, but it's the men who miss the former affection of their partner. Of course, not every man makes a big deal out of it, and it doesn't mean that there aren't women who miss the familiar closeness with their partner. In any case, you need to talk about it because your relationship is also important for your baby. If one of you wants more togetherness, you should agree to it. Agree on arrangements that suit you both. Your baby will sense your positive attitude towards one another.

WHEN CAN I START LETTING A BABYSITTER WATCH MY CHILD?

From a practical point of view, there's nothing wrong with entrusting your baby to a babysitter immediately after birth. Whether it's desirable is another story. In the beginning, it's very important for you and your baby to spend a lot of time together. You have to get used to one another, which doesn't happen overnight. It really is best for your baby to feel your presence as often as possible. That way, you form a tight bond, and you give your baby the basic feeling of security and comfort. "As often as possible" is difficult to define, though. What is "as often as possible?" On the one hand, your baby is the highest priority. On the other hand, there are things that you can't do when your baby is with you or you have critical obligations. In this case, you don't have a choice but to entrust your baby to a babysitter.

Sleep

- Do you always bring your baby to bed at the same time whether the baby is tired or not?
- If the baby doesn't want to sleep, after how many minutes should you go and get him or her?
- Should you stay in your baby's room until the little one is asleep?
- Do you think you spoil your baby if you respond to his or her crying?
- Who brings the baby to bed?
- Who gets up at night if the baby cries?
- How about whoever gets up at night the most during the week gets to stay in bed on weekends?
- Should breast milk be expressed, so Mom doesn't always have to get up and can sleep through the night every now and then?
- Is there someone living close by who could come by every once in a while for an hour, so you can take a powernap during the day?

Crying

- Do you let your baby cry every now and then?
- Do you both agree on the extent of comfort?
- Do you both agree on the way of comforting?
- When it comes to comforting, what are the differences between you and your partner, and could you learn something from one another?
- Do you both think that you really have to be there for your baby when the little one is going through a difficult phase even though it's sometimes at the expense of the attention you pay to yourself or your partner?

○ Do you both agree that your baby cries more due to a leap, or does one of you doubt the reason for crying? (When in doubt, always contact a doctor or consultation center.)

Diet

○ Do you both agree on the food your baby gets (breast or bottle)?

○ If you breastfeed, have you discussed what this means for a mother?

○ If you breastfeed, does your partner know that this may be a physically difficult task?

○ If you breastfeed, is there something your partner can do to help with feeding?

○ Are you unsure if your baby takes in enough food? (When in doubt, always ask a doctor.)

○ Do you agree on the amount of solid food you give your baby?

○ Do you agree on how to handle your baby's refusal to eat during a leap?

Stress Relief

○ Do you both agree that the stress is due to a leap? (When in doubt, contact a doctor or consultation center.)

○ When it comes to parenting, are the responsibilities evenly distributed?

○ Do you agree that raising children uses up a lot of energy even when they're still very young?

○ Is it an option that your partner spends more time with the baby when he or she is getting to be too much for you?

DOES EVERY LEAP HAVE A BIG IMPACT ON THE WHOLE FAMILY?

Not every leap has the same effect on every baby. The first leaps happen quickly and have smaller impacts on the family than the following leaps. The older your baby gets, the longer the leaps last. Therefore, the periods of time during which your child doesn't sleep will last longer, too. Nevertheless, even the first leaps may tarnish domestic harmony, especially since you don't have any experience being that it's your first baby, are insecure, doubt yourself, or worry about your baby's health. Doubts bring along stress and affect the other family members.

CAN I PREPARE MY OTHER CHILDREN FOR OUR BABY'S LEAP?

It makes sense that your baby's leap is implicitly difficult for the other children as well. Depending on the siblings' age, you might be able explain to them what's going on with your baby. Starting at the age of four years, children understand this. It is best is to come up with a little story about what's changing in the baby's head. Of course, you don't need to explain every little detail because this would be too difficult for a child to understand. However, the child understands that the baby has to learn a lot right now, and that's why the baby's whole world is changing at the moment. Your children can even help out. For instance, ask the older children to help you distract or comfort the baby by drawing or crafting something for the little one.

HOW CAN I MAKE SURE THAT MY INCREASED ATTENTION TO MY BABY IS NOT AT MY OTHER CHILDREN'S EXPENSE?

Spreading time and devotion evenly is an art of its own. More than likely, you'll hear from your older children that you're doing it wrong, no matter how hard you try. The oldest will complain that you're constantly busy with the baby while the younger ones become whiny again in order to get your attention. Try to make your baby a part of the games you played with your other children before the baby was born. Your baby loves being involved when you're doing crafts with the other children. Carry the little one in a sling or put the bouncer next to you. While you're taking your time crafting with your other children, talk to your baby often and show him or her the crafts you're making. That way, your older children don't have a reason to protest since you're spending time with them, too. Your baby enjoys being a part of and watching a happy group. You can even incorporate leaps into these activities. For example, when showing your baby the craft you're working on, carefully use it to fan the little one; that way, you incorporate the leap of "smooth transitions" (at about 12 weeks of age). Or you could take a piece of paper and make a rustling sound while allowing the baby to feel how it crackles during the leap of "events" (at about 19 weeks of age). If your baby is currently trying to sit, place the little one next to you with the support of your nursing pillow. That way, you'll have your hands free to craft while your baby is having fun learning to sit. You see, with a little creativity, you're able to please everyone!

HOW DO I EXPLAIN TO MY OTHER CHILDREN THAT THE BABY IS ALLOWED TO DO CERTAIN THINGS THAT THEY AREN'T ALLOWED TO DO?

Starting at the age of 18 months, a child realizes that there are differences and that the little brother or sister is sometimes allowed to do something that he or she is not allowed to do. Although the child's brain is able to understand this, it doesn't necessarily mean that he or she agrees to the fact. Explain to your other children that the baby is not as far in development as they are, so you expect more from them than from a little baby. Repeat this message clearly during every discussion.

HOW DO I HANDLE IT WHEN MY IN-LAWS' OPINIONS REGARDING PARENTING ARE DIFFERENT FROM MINE?

When your parents or in-laws were raising their children, they did it their way. Now that you have children, you do it your way. When it comes to parenting, the important thing is that everyone does it the way that works for them. Go ahead and take good advice from parents who are a little more experienced, but don't let it get to you. In the past, only one generation earlier, crying was shrugged off as belly cramps, a baby was fed at set times instead of on demand, and much less was known about a baby's mental development. In recent years, lots of research has been done regarding the development of babies. Nowadays, we know significantly more. However, for some reason, many grandparents feel the need to voice their unsolicited opinion. It's really absurd considering that their parents probably got on their nerves doing the same thing. Take the advice calmly. Avoid these discussions when possible, but when they do occur, deal with the advice however you please. Realize that the advisors probably want the same thing for your baby as you do: only the best.

MY PARENTS WATCH MY BABY BUT DO THINGS I ABSOLUTELY DON'T WANT THEM TO DO. HOW SHOULD I MAKE IT CLEAR TO THEM?

Usually, it is easier to express your concerns to a babysitter or a caretaker when there's something you don't agree with. After all, you are the parents and are entitled to make the decisions. It's a little bit more delicate if your parents are doing something that you don't agree with while watching the baby. The older generation has their own idea when it comes to parenting, and if you criticize, you indicate that something was wrong with the way you were raised. However, it is important to hold on to your personal principles regarding raising your baby. Explain to your parents that society has changed; thus, there have been changes in parenting as well. That way, they do not feel attacked. You won't be able to blame everything on social changes, though; this is when you need to remain steadfast with your opinion. If there are serious differences, you may want to ask yourself whether or not you'd be better off looking for another babysitter.

Chapter 8

INTELLIGENCE

Interests, Personality,
Thinking, Stimulating,
and Support

As parents, you want the best for your baby. You're secretly hoping for an intelligent child with a successful future in store. What is intelligence, though? Does intelligence really have something to do with success, and how do you assess the baby's preferences and interests? Even more importantly, is it really necessary for parents to focus on the baby's preferences and interests?

WHAT IS INTELLIGENCE?

Intelligence is a big word that's actually often used incorrectly. At the mentioning of the word, intelligence quotients and the according good grades in school come to mind. True intelligence, of course, goes way beyond success in school. Today, we know with increasing certainty that there is not only one form of intelligence but multiple forms. The founder of this theory is Howard Gardner. According to him, there are eight different forms of intelligence:

1 Musical intelligence

2 Bodily-kinesthetic intelligence (the ability to utilize the body or parts of the body when playing, performing in various kinds of sports, or expressing emotions as in ballet or dance)

3 Logical-mathematical intelligence (talented at math)

4 Linguistic intelligence

5 Spatial intelligence (the ability to think in three dimensions or spatial overview)

6 Interpersonal or social intelligence (the ability to recognize intentions and desires of others even when not said out loud)

7 Intrapersonal intelligence (the ability to understand one's own feelings and use them to direct actions)

8 Naturalist intelligence (the ability to understand animals and plants in a special way)

DOES A BABY HAVE ALL THE FORMS OF INTELLIGENCE?

Your baby has every form of intelligence within him- or herself. The question is which forms are most developed. Starting at birth, your baby has an inclination for one or several forms of intelligence. This will become more and more obvious to you the older the baby gets. However, it's still a little early to use the word, "intelligence." In babies and young children, it's better to speak of interests and skills. You are more likely able to make use of the terms, "interests" and "skills." With your ability to recognize your baby's interests and focus on the stimulation of those interests, your baby will easily develop inherent talents. The intention is not to turn your baby into a smart child but into a happy one. Your baby wants to be supported in the things he or she is fascinated with and interested in, just like everyone else.

WHY IS IT SO IMPORTANT THAT I PAY ATTENTION TO MY CHILD'S INTERESTS?

During the first few years, you and your child get to know each other. If you observe carefully, the baby's unique personality will reveal itself to you with increasing clarity, and this is, without a doubt, the most beautiful "expedition" you'll ever go on in your life. Part of the personality you'll get to know on this expedition is your baby's interests. They play a role in determining the way of development, including how the baby handles leaps, masters skills, and accepts new challenges. You see, your baby's interests are certainly one of the most important aspects regarding what needs to be focused on during development since they determine how the various forms of intelligence develop. Always keep in mind that the baby is the one who has to find the interests, and they may not necessarily coincide with yours. Let your child show you what he or she is interested in, and don't force anything on the child that you like. It sounds like it would go without saying, but it's actually one of the most difficult things in parenting.

HOW CAN I DETERMINE MY CHILD'S INTERESTS AND SKILLS?

After every leap, your child receives another new perceptive ability, which results in the development of many new skills. The child subconsciously chooses what to master first. What the child chooses reveals his or her interests and skills, and therefore, it reveals something about his or her personality. After a few leaps, you'll notice that your baby is always most interested in the same kind of skills. For one child, it may be all motor skills (bodily-kinesthetic), and for another, it could be interpersonal interests and the appertaining games. It is too early, though, to draw conclusions for later life, especially since your baby is still in the midst of developing. However, keep the apparent interests in mind and respond to them by playing games with your child according to the interests.

HOW DO I KNOW WHAT MY CHILD IS ALREADY ABLE TO DO AND UNDERSTAND AND WHAT IS STILL TOO DIFFICULT?

People are the most content when there's balance in life and when there's no boredom. At the same time, they don't like having to do things that are too difficult and demanding. Your child wants to be approached on his or her level. You do your child the biggest favor by being aware of the level of development and by responding accordingly. Take your time to get to know your child and observe carefully. The older the child gets, the more you'll notice that the little one sometimes gets bored with something and longs for a new challenge. On the flip side, you may notice that your child is frustrated because of things he or she doesn't understand or is unable to do. The more you devote yourself to your child, the better you'll figure out his or her interests and abilities. You'll also discover what's considered a welcomed challenge, what's too difficult of a task, what's too easy and boring, and what the child doesn't want to do anymore.

Tip

Never demand too much of your child, no matter the age. Appreciate your child the way he or she is. Always ask for things your child is able to do, and stimulate in a way that meets the child's interests.

IS THERE A WAY TO FIND OUT WHETHER MY CHILD WILL HAVE A HIGH IQ LATER IN LIFE?

There is no checklist that can help you determine early on what intelligence quotient your child will have at the age of six or older, which is good. However, there's research being done on how this form of intelligence can be predicted at an early age. In the course of the research, circumstances have been discovered suggesting that it may be predictable whether a baby will be highly intelligent or skilled later in life based on a number of indicators.

Your baby:

○ Is demanding and not easily satisfied

○ Cries a lot (also see Chapter 4, "Crying," page 73)

○ Is easily bored

○ Is constantly searching for a new challenge

○ Is able to be occupied with something in deep concentration for a long time

○ Observes a lot

○ "Practices" in his or her head

○ Is predominantly successful on the first try when trying something new

○ Demands more attention than other babies

○ Has highly developed fine motor skills on his or her level (also see Chapter 2, "Physical Development," page 33)

Always keep in mind that these are solely indicators. Not every demanding baby possesses a high intelligence and vice versa. Parents are better off trusting their intuition and simply keeping these indicators in mind.

CAN LITTLE BABIES BE DEMANDING?

Everyone knows that newborn babies do not sleep around the clock to give parents a chance to do what they want, unlike what stories suggest. The fact is that only very few newborn babies sleep eight hours at a time and lie peacefully in their little beds during the time when they're awake. Most parents have the feeling that their baby shows his or her needs soon after birth. The baby wants to be held, to be nursed (without being hungry), and to look at the surroundings and is bored when he or she is in the same spot for too long. You'll notice it even more after the first leap, which occurs approximately five weeks after the calculated delivery date. With every leap, your baby wants to learn more about life, and this is how it's supposed to be. Therefore, it's perfectly normal that you realize your baby demands more and more. However, there are babies that clearly demand much more than usual after a leap and the respective age. The parents, then, feel like they're on their last leg and are desperately searching all day long for ways to satisfy their baby. They discover, for instance, that the baby is very interested in a certain picture in the room. For five minutes, the baby looks at the picture with big

eyes, finally seems to be happy, and falls asleep. Upon waking and becoming restless, the picture is suddenly not interesting anymore. The parents, once again, have to go in search for something else that may be interesting. It, then, seems as if the baby had looked at the picture, processed it in the brain, and "put it aside." The baby needs new stimulation and stays restless until being offered something new that's interesting. Babies like this are called demanding. To a lot of people, the word, "demanding," has a negative ring, but it really should be an inspiring, nice challenge for parents to raise a child who wants to get everything out of life that it has to offer. This is actually great, isn't it?

HOW DO YOU PREVENT BOREDOM IN BABIES?

All babies want to learn. They want to discover the world. They are fascinated with anything new to them. If your baby gets bored, it just means that the little one is telling you that "I understand this already, and now, I'd like to see or experience something different." Some babies' boredom is more obvious than others', and they cry and become restless. That's your signal that your baby is looking for a new challenge. Other babies make it less obvious that they're bored and may become somewhat withdrawn. It's especially important for parents of these babies to interpret the behavior correctly. Just because a baby is not clearly showing interest in new things doesn't mean that the little one doesn't have a desire for them; the desire is definitely there! Explore together what the child is fascinated with, wants to discover, feels like doing, and wants to be challenged with.

HOW DO I FIND OUT WHAT STIMULATES MY BABY?

First of all, you need to get to know your baby well. Over time, you will find out what the baby is fascinated with, what's boring, and what's still too difficult and challenging. You'll never know with 100 percent certainty, no matter how hard you try. Your baby develops quickly, and factors stimulating the baby to master certain skills change just as quickly. However, this is what makes the whole thing so enjoyable for you and your baby. Basically, the whole family is busy discovering all the new things with the baby. For instance, your baby finds out that a rubber ball bounces and moves up and down. Something you took for granted is a fun game to the baby, and the baby's excitement over the bouncing ball transfers to you. Because of your baby, you get to know the world in a new way.

By delving into the leap your baby is currently going through, you'll get clues regarding the challenges your baby will pursue. You are informed about what's going on in his or her little head and what new skills come with the leap. So one week before your baby takes a leap, read the pertaining chapter in this book. Start thinking about what your baby is about to learn. Contemplate whether the conditions at home are right to implement the leap or if you need to do or change something beforehand. By preparing for the leap and adjusting to what your baby is fascinated with during this phase and what stimulates his or her interests, it will be easier for your baby to accomplish the leap.

HOW DO I FIND THE RIGHT AMOUNT OF CHALLENGE FOR MY BABY?

A child wants to be challenged on his or her level in an appealing way. If the bar is set to high or low, the baby gets frustrated. If you force a way of playing on the child that doesn't match the child's personality, don't be surprised when the child isn't participating with excitement. Your baby is the one deciding whether a new challenge is welcome or not. If you push too hard and try to stimulate too much, which demands too much from your child, the consequences are negative rather than positive. This actually applies to everything regarding development. Don't offer anything; instead, let your child choose. Don't force anything on the child that's not interesting or that's too difficult.

WHY DOES MY BABY SUDDENLY SEEM STARTLED OR FRIGHTENED BY SOMETHING THAT'S ACTUALLY FASCINATING TO HIM OR HER?

Your baby is interested in anything new. The new thing is something the baby suddenly understands due to the leap that enabled the little one to understand it. The new thing is challenging, and at the same time, a new world opens up to the baby. The child's interest is aroused because the brain longs to discover new things. It's still perfectly normal if your baby seems to be reluctant or afraid of the new thing now and then. The baby is more or less aware of not really knowing the game that's being played or the feeling he or she suddenly has.

Your baby senses so many new impressions that he or she is being assaulted by and becomes afraid of or startled by the new things. Most often, you don't see it in a fearful reaction, but the child closes his or her eyes or looks away. The little one needs a brief, quiet moment to process it. If you notice this reaction in your baby, let the little one have that moment. Also, leave it to your baby to show you when he or she has had enough rest. Sometimes, it's only a few seconds; other times, it takes longer. Your baby knows exactly how much time is needed to process the new impressions, so let the baby lead you.

IS IT UNUSUAL THAT A BABY IS COMPLETELY FASCINATED WITH SOMETHING AND CAN'T GET ANY REST BECAUSE OF IT?

Most babies clearly show when rest is needed. The new game is fun to them, but when they are getting tired, they give in to fatigue. However, after having accomplished a leap, some babies are so interested in their new skills that they want to try out everything at all costs and keep going until they achieve their goal and master the new skills. These babies demand a lot from their parents but also demand a lot from themselves. That's why they sometimes need to be protected from themselves. Try to find situations that allow your baby to engage in the new skills that come with a leap but also to calm down.

IS IT NORMAL THAT MY BABY IS OCCUPIED FOR HOURS AT A TIME WITH SOMETHING IRRELEVANT?

What seems irrelevant to us may be tremendously interesting to a baby. You're not the first parent to discover that the fancy toy with all the different functions is exciting to the baby because of the label that's stuck to it. Your baby has an eye for detail. The little one may be vastly fascinated by the most irrelevant things. Since these may be trivial to us, some parents think that their baby is dull. Some even draw the conclusion that their baby is autistic because the little one steadily strokes a step with his or her little fingers or keeps twisting a reel of thread for hours at a time. Parents are inclined to assume the worst, but there's hardly ever a reason for it. Being occupied with something trivial for hours at a time is certainly no reason to doubt your child's intelligence or health. It's quite the opposite; the baby's brain is working hard. The baby discovers the world's basic laws. For example, by stroking the step, the baby familiarizes him- or herself with the material and his or her surroundings and also experiences the fundamental forces at that moment by moving his or

her finger across a certain spot. By twisting a reel of thread, which involves making very subtle movements with the hand, the baby allows something to look different. We know that something looks different from a different angle even though it's still the same thing. Your baby is discovering this while twisting the reel. This is actually clever!

IS THE BRAIN BEING STIMULATED WHEN THE BABY IS BEING TALKED TO A LOT?

Your baby enjoys your dialogue even at a very young age. The little one listens to your voice and looks at your face. This is calming and comforting to the baby. With these intense "conversations," the baby practices seeing, hearing, listening, smelling, and moving. Talk to your baby as often as possible, and start this right after birth because soon after birth, quick neuronal branching takes place in the cerebrum. The more connections, the better the transmission of information. By talking to your child a lot, you stimulate interaction, and this interaction ensures that the connections will be preserved. As crazy as it may sound, the newly formed connections can die off if not used.

IS A BABY'S BRAIN STIMULATED BY EXPOSING THE BABY TO MANY NEW EXPERIENCES?

As a matter of fact, your baby longs for new experiences. Nobody is as curious and eager to learn as a baby. Animal studies have shown that neuronal connections form when stimulated by experiences early on. We are using the term, "experiences," in the widest sense of the word. It's about the baby hearing, seeing, and experiencing new things. In the past, it was assumed that very young babies are not able to do anything; therefore, they were left for hours at a time in their little beds without any attention. The common way of thinking was that babies aren't able to learn, yet. Nowadays, we know better. Therefore, talk to your baby, let the little one embrace the surroundings, react to your baby's signals, and let the baby be a part of your family and everyday activities as much as possible. That way, you stimulate formation of neuronal connections in the brain. Think of it this way: you'll get back double and triple the energy you invest in the form of an active and happy child who's eager to learn. By putting your baby aside all the time without interaction, you raise a child who does not want to do anything and who hardly interacts.

DOES THE WAY I TREAT MY BABY HAVE ANY EFFECT ON HIS OR HER IQ LATER IN LIFE?

In fact, the intelligence quotient is partially influenced by the way you treat your baby. For the most part, it is determined at the time of conception, and there is clear evidence that IQ is hereditary. However, you are able to influence it positively as well as negatively, and it starts with pregnancy. As is already known, smoking is not only harmful to you and your baby's health, but it also has an immediate negative effect on the baby's IQ. The same applies for the time after birth because the baby takes in harmful substances when drinking breast milk and breathing in the smoke. Besides physical impacts, the amount of stimulation you provide early on plays a role in IQ as well. This is proven by a study done on children in a day care center where caregivers did hardly anything or even nothing at all with the babies. They didn't pay much attention to the babies, who were mainly lying in their little beds staring at a boring white ceiling. Years later, when the children's IQ was measured, it was indeed lower than in another group of babies that were sufficiently stimulated.

DOES GOING TO A DAY CARE CENTER HAVE AN INFLUENCE ON HIS OR HER IQ?

Everything and everyone taking care of your baby influences the baby's development, including IQ and how much stimulation is being provided to develop the baby's interests. A bad day care center has a certain impact on our baby's development. However, the same applies to a babysitter or even you! Getting everything he or she needs from every direction is very important for your baby, including experiences with the surroundings and the time the baby needs to discover them. It's more difficult when you entrust your baby to a babysitter or a day care center. Sometimes, your child is treated differently than you would like. Discuss your concerns with the manager of the day care center or with the babysitter, and try to work out a plan. If you realize that you can't come to an agreement, you are better off looking for another babysitter or day care center even if this creates logistic problems. Your baby is more important.

AT WHAT POINT DOES A BABY START THINKING CONSCIOUSLY?

"Consciously" is a very difficult term. Even in adults, "consciously" can't really be described. If you think about it in terms of "purposefully," it's a little easier to understand. With every leap in development, the baby continuously sets more complex goals. The purposefulness is increasingly similar to ours. In the past, a baby was considered to be born barren, which means a body consisting of bones and muscles with skin around them that's equipped with a few reflexes. Fortunately nowadays, we know better. Starting with day one, your baby has a simple way of purposefulness.

Chapter 9

PARENTING

Rules, Boundaries, Whining,
Demanding, Learning, Social
Behavior, and Punishing

The older your baby gets, the more the "self" emerges. You increasingly see the baby's personality come to light, which fills you with happiness. However, there are moments when the child's interests are not the same as yours. Your child will test your limits, and it's up to you to set boundaries and teach the child rules, not to make life difficult for the child but because children need rules when growing up. By providing sensible rules, you're making sure that the child has a good start at the day care center, in school, and later in life.

AT WHAT AGE DO YOU HAVE TO SET BOUNDARIES?

Once your baby has completed the leap of "principles" (64 weeks after the calculated due date or almost 15 months), you can and must teach the child rules. "Must" isn't a pretty word; however, it's appropriate. The child needs to learn rules in order to be able to lead a pleasant life in society. In fact, the child wants to learn rules even though it doesn't seem like it with all the whining.

IS A BABY UNDER THE AGE OF 15 MONTHS NOT ABLE TO LEARN ANY RULES?

As long has the leap of "principles" hasn't been accomplished, you may lead by example and correct your baby the moment he or she does something "wrong." You may, for example, plainly say, "No, don't do that!" when the baby pulls on you or when you take something away that the baby is not allowed to have. That way, you correct your little one in the course of the game he or she is playing. Be sure to enforce the rules immediately. Once the leap of "principles" is complete, the child suddenly understands that he or she may get his or her way by acting very sweetly, by helping you, or, on the contrary, by whining. At this age, the child already understands that certain behaviors can help him or her get what he or she wants. That's when the time has come to lay down clear rules.

HOW CAN I KEEP MY CHILD FROM WHINING?

Every child whines, and it's simply a part of life. One child may whine more than another. A vivacious child expresses his or her will more than a quiet child. However, disposition is not the only factor in deciding whether your child will act like a little troublemaker every now and then. Your role is very important, too. If you don't take consistent action, your child will, no doubt, take advantage of it. Not taking consistent action in setting rules means that something that's forbidden sometimes is also allowed other times. It won't take your child long at all to figure out when something can be achieved with whining because you're emitting signals. By being consistent, you don't prevent your child from whining, but you're ensuring that it happens less often and for a shorter time.

SOMETIMES, THE WHINING JUST DOESN'T STOP. WHAT DO I DO THEN?

At a first glance, enforcing the rules on a consistent basis seems easy. After all, adults know what's allowed and what isn't, and you would think it could be made clear to a child, too. This is as far as the theory goes. In reality, it's easy to be tempted to give in to the child's whining because other people are bothered, because you're in a hurry, or because you can't stand listening to it any longer. However, it is recommended to stay consistent, especially in these situations. If you give in just once, your child will remember and take advantage of you next time.

IF ALL CHILDREN WHINE ANYWAY, WHAT GOOD DOES IT DO TO ENFORCE THE RULES CONSISTENTLY?

Your child is at an age now where he or she develops an increasingly stronger will. After the leap of "systems" (around the age of 17 months), the child is a person with an opinion and rights. That's a good development because the child increasingly develops a "self" that fits into society. Every human being is a social creature that wants to belong to a group and be respected by that group. A "sweet" child is more easily accepted than a "naughty" child, just to name two extremes. It's your job to raise your child to get along well with others; the child needs to be able to adapt within a group and know what's allowed and what isn't. Whining is normal and is part of your child's development, but don't let this be an excuse to not take action in hopes that it will pass on its own.

IS IT POSSIBLE TO RAISE MY CHILD TO WHERE THERE'S NO WHINING LATER ON?

Your child will whine less if you only ask him or her to do what he or she is fully capable of doing from day one. That way, you subconsciously teach the child that you are expecting something from him or her. With every leap, your baby acquires a new perceptive ability, enabling the little one to do and understand something new. This is the child's highest level of understanding at the moment. Once the leap has been accomplished, you may ask that your child use the enhanced perceptive ability. If you expect more from your child than the ability allows, the child will become frustrated and the task won't become easier. It will be quite the opposite; the child will whine more often and longer.

HOW DOES MY CHILD ALWAYS KNOWS EXACTLY WHEN WHINING WORKS?

During the past months, you and your baby have become closer and closer. Once your child is between one and two years old, the little one knows you inside and out. The child knows exactly what you like, what's funny to you, and what you're sensitive to. A child at that age uses this knowledge ruthlessly, no matter how pleasant-natured the child is. The little one senses the exact moment you're tempted to give in. You must become aware of these moments. Think of the situations when you give in to your child's whining. Is it at the supermarket because you're embarrassed? Or is it when your child acts very sweetly and showers you with kisses? Or is it when you're busy cooking, the other children are causing trouble, and the dog is looking at you with begging eyes? Once you're aware of when and why you break down, the danger of being caught off guard decreases, and you'll be able to react in time. For instance, you shouldn't allow your child to have his or her way while strangers are present because you're embarrassed of your child's behavior. You should react to your child's behavior instead of worrying about what the stranger thinks.

SHOULD A BABYSITTER ENFORCE THE SAME RULES THE PARENTS SET?

Being consistent is very important when it comes to parenting. Your 15-month-old child doesn't quite understand yet that Dad allows something that Mom doesn't allow. The message you're giving your child is that rules only apply in certain situations, so test them to see if you can get away with it. This is too difficult for your child; you're asking too much of the little one. That's why it's best for you and your partner to agree to the rules and consistently enforce them. The same applies for the babysitter. Everyone in charge of raising your child has to be on the same page. This is the only way to be consistent.

WHEN AM I ALLOWED TO BE MORE FLEXIBLE WITH THE RULES?

Exceptions confirm the rule. However, exceptions also create confusion for your child. A child doesn't understand such subtlety regarding consistency until he or she is older than two years. At this time, you may explain that sometimes you make an exception to a rule, including allowing the child to have a snack at a party or to stay up longer on the weekends. Always clearly explain to your child that it's an exception. Tell the little one that something is allowed this one time, and also explain why you're making an exception. Observe the way the child handles it. Does the child understand that it's an exception, or does the little one start whining to enforce more exceptions? Adjust the frequency of exceptions to the child's reactions.

WHAT IS THE LONG-TERM EFFECT OF CONSISTENTLY ENFORCING THE RULES?

Teaching a 15-month-old child the rules regarding what's appropriate and what isn't is one of the best premises to raise a child that knows and observes social values and standards. A child raised in this way will be self-confident when starting school and will fit in easily. The parents don't have to worry when their child goes to a friend's house to play because they know the child will behave. In short, the parents will be proud of their child. Children between the age of one and two years who haven't been taught rules whine more often and for longer periods of time. It gets even worse at the age of four years and older. You can read many stories about aggressive children who throw tantrums, break things, and hurt others intentionally. These are the consequences when you don't take parenting seriously. And it's certainly not what parents wish for.

IS IT OKAY TO PUNISH A BABY?

A baby has no way of knowing that he or she is doing something "wrong." All you may say is, "No, this hurts," or something along these lines and use facial expressions and reactions to make your displeasure clear. If your baby does the same thing again 10 minutes later, repeat what you said earlier and show the same reaction. A baby wouldn't understand what he or she is being punished for, and punishing a baby wouldn't be appropriate for that reason alone.

Starting with the age of 15 months, it's a different story. The child now understands that there are rules, and the little one has to take responsibility when testing the rules. Testing the rules by defying them multiple times is perfectly normal at this age. That way, the child learns the rules. If you'd like to "punish" your child because the little one is testing a rule, by no means should it be done in the form of yelling, hitting, or by using any other form of physical or verbal force. By doing so, you only show your own weakness. However, you certainly may discipline your child at this age by showing and letting the little one emotionally feel that you don't accept the behavior. For instance, if the child takes a candleholder from the table, tell the child that this is not allowed. Does the child reach for the candleholder once again? Pick the child up and put him or her somewhere else in the room. Always tell your child why something is not allowed at eye level. Look at your child and try to distract the child afterwards with a different, "desirable" action.

HOW DO I MAKE IT CLEAR TO A CHILD THAT SOMETHING IS NOT ALLOWED?

Words alone aren't enough, unfortunately, but neither are actions. You can tell your child a hundred times that climbing this or that is not allowed, but if you do so while laughing and with a friendly face while you stay seated on the couch, your protests won't make a big impression on your child, who will just carry on. Use verbal and nonverbal communication to make rules clear, including words, posture, and actions. It's about your facial expressions and posture in addition to telling your child. Laugh when you're happy, and make an angry face when you're irritated. It sounds like it would go without saying, but many people aren't aware of their expressions when talking. It's very important that your face and posture clearly show your current feeling, especially with a child. A little exaggeration doesn't hurt, either. Sometimes, parents have to do a little bit of acting. Besides posture and facial expressions, you also have to consider the level you're standing or sitting on. If you want your message to really get across, you need to look straight at your child. Get on the same eye level, and look him or her in the eye. That way, you drive the point home.

SOMETIMES, I HAVE TO LAUGH OUT LOUD WHEN MY CHILD DOES SOMETHING NAUGHTY. IS THIS WRONG?

Fortunately, our children's behavior often makes us laugh, for example, when a child tries to secretly do something in an obvious manner. Let's be honest; something naughty is actually sometimes funny. Even whining may be downright funny. However, if you laugh, your child takes it as doing the right thing. Laughing means praising, so try to not laugh, no matter how difficult it may be. Also, ask your older children not to laugh when the baby misbehaves. Since it's even harder for children to suppress their laughter, tell them that it may be best for them to go to another room for a little while.

CAN A TODDLER BE AGGRESSIVE?

Yes, a toddler can be aggressive. It's not unusual. Actually, almost all children at the age of one to two years show aggressive behavior. Of course, you have to understand the term, "aggressive behavior," in the broadest sense. Most often, you'll realize that the child suddenly shows aggressive behavior more frequently after the leap of "principles" (around the age of 15 months). Examples of aggressive behavior might include the child biting something very hard, hitting something, or intentionally knocking something down and looking at you as if wanting to test you. That's exactly what the child is doing, not to make your life difficult for you but because the little one experiments with social behavior after this leap. The child tries to judge whether the behavior is right or wrong by looking at your reaction. Your child is getting to know life, and you're there to teach the little one life and the rules that come with it.

DO PARENTS HAVE ANY INFLUENCE ON AGGRESSIVE BEHAVIOR?

Every child experiments with aggression. Ninety percent of all 17-month-old babies show occasional aggressive behavior. Most often, experimenting with aggression has topped out by the time the child turns two, and it continues to decrease from that point on. Once your child starts elementary school, this phase is over or is at least under normal circumstances. Although a certain degree of aggression is normal, it is never acceptable. Make this clear to your child. Always lead by example. If you yell and scream when arguing with your partner, you can't expect your child to solve conflicts any other way. When the child is angry, he or she screams, too, and maybe screams even louder than you. If you slam doors when you're mad, your child will probably throw things when he or she is angry. You're the child's role model, and you subconsciously teach your child how to act with your behavior. A child that grows up in a family where aggression is a part of everyday life will continue with this behavior when most other children don't show aggression anymore.

MY CHILD NEVER WHINES WHEN WANTING SOMETHING BUT IS EXTREMELY SWEET INSTEAD. HOW AM I SUPPOSED TO SAY "NO?"

Some children find out early on that it's easier to catch flies with honey than with vinegar. They choose a strategy other than whining to get their way. They look at you sweetly with big eyes, help you, and cuddle with you; they play the sweet child. However, this behavior has the same purpose as whining. Both are methods for children to get their way. The only difference is that whining is more annoying. Teach your child that some things are not allowed, no matter how nice he or she acts. Rules are rules.